# SPARKED

## Rebellious Leadership Beyond the Ordinary

HUGO PÉREZ

Ballast Books, LLC
www.ballastbooks.com



ISBN: 978-1-966786-92-4

Printed in the United States of America

Published by Ballast Books
www.ballastbooks.com

For more information, bulk orders, appearances, or speaking requests, please email: info@ballastbooks.com

# DEDICATION

This book is for the storytellers and the dreamers.
The rule-breakers and bridge-builders.
The wild ones with soft hearts and sharp minds.
The roaring lambs who refuse to go quiet.

It's for anyone who's ever felt the spark and wondered if it was safe to let it burn.

And it's for my daily reminders of what a life fully lit can look like—my nephews and nieces, both blood and chosen, my living proof that the future is still worth fighting for:

*Thelo, Nico, Nila, Oren, Naiomy, Levi, Emilia, Owen, Eliza, Ezra, Elias, Esai, Malachi, Isaac, Reyna, Reuben, Raphi, Koen, Maggie, and Noah.*

May you never dim.
May you never need to apologize for your fire.
May you always choose courage over comfort.

Above all, this book is for the original rebel—the woman who taught me how to lean in, speak up, and spark the fire even when the world said, "Stay small."

*Mami.*

Everything starts with you.

# SPARKED

Rebellious Leadership Beyond the Ordinary

# TABLE OF CONTENTS

INTRO

# FUEL, FIRE, AND THE AUDACITY TO BE YOU!

Let's get one thing straight from the jump: I'm a truth-teller. Always have been.

I lead with transparency. I speak with fire. And while my compassion runs deep and my emotional IQ is dialed in, my tolerance for sugarcoating? Practically nonexistent.

Sorry. *Not sorry.*

You'll feel that all over this book.

The rhythm might punch. The tone might swerve. And yes, a few spicy words might slip in here and there—not because I talk like that 24/7 but because sometimes, frankly, only a well-placed "hell yes" or "damn" gets the point across with the heat it deserves. Call it intentional rebellion, not reckless profanity.

This isn't a manual. It's a manifesto.

This is for the leaders who don't fit the mold, who ask better questions, who challenge tired narratives, and who feel deep in their gut that there's got to be a more honest, human, courageous way to lead.

If you've ever been told you were too much, too different, too loud, too emotional, too real—*good*. You're exactly who this book was written for.

It's not that I don't want to guide you gently toward some enlightening transformation. (Okay, let's be honest—I *really* don't want to do that.) It's more a realization that what we don't need more of right now is motivational fluff wrapped in TED Talk lingo helping you check off the list of accomplishments on your way to becoming who you want to be.

Instead, what's coming your way is raw. It's lived in. It's bold. Because that's what I know and what I've gone through. And frankly, it's what it takes to live a sparked life in a world that keeps trying to smother the flame.

This book didn't come from strategy. It *tumbled* out of me like it already knew its destination. Real, loud, uninvited after a sharp, unexpected end to a job I loved.

I was serving as chief marketing officer for a company doing bold, disruptive work, stuff I believed in. But one day, in a jagged, jarring pivot, the owners decided they were done. Not with *me*—but with the *fight*. They didn't want to keep investing in the messy, expensive, long-game work it would take to win in the marketplace. They pulled the plug.

And just like that . . . I was done.

No soft landing. No exit plan. Just me . . . and the mirror.

What followed wasn't some hustle culture reinvention arc or perfectly curated LinkedIn comeback.

It was quiet. Restless. Disorienting.

I found myself yanking on threads—of identity, of leadership, of meaning. What had I *actually* learned? What kind of leader was I beneath the job titles? Who was I *really*? And who had I always been but hadn't dared to own?

And somewhere in the chaos, something cracked open. What came pouring out wasn't bitterness. It wasn't a rebrand.

It was this book.

Not a personal catharsis. Not a résumé booster. But a war drum. A guide. A mirror for anyone who's sick of playing small.

Because here's what I realized: My life has been shaped not by the moments that look good in a bio but by the ones that *scarred* me, *enlightened* me, *forged* me.

Like the childhood ritual of cramming into the middle seat between my brothers in my mom's beat-up car, weaving through morning traffic from our home in Chicago's Humboldt Park to a far-flung North Side school. Why? Because my mom—an educator with zero tolerance for mediocrity—refused to let geography dictate my future.

She didn't ask for permission. She *demanded* opportunity.

She got me into a program that wasn't built for kids like me. She didn't care what was "typical." She cared what was *possible*. Every car ride was a sacrifice. A statement. A protest on wheels.

And the soundtrack?

Spanish radio dramas, filled with plot twists, passion, heartbreak, blasting from the dashboard. I didn't know it at the time, but I was learning tone, tempo, storytelling, and fire. That car became a classroom. A chapel. A crucible.

But the real plot twist came later.

First day of sixth grade. The teacher was doing that awkward, get-to-know-you intro round.

That's when a girl stood up—pink dress, raised chin, fierce smile—and said, "My name is Cielo. It means 'sky.'" Just context. Not permission.

The class responded instinctively: "Hello, Cielo!"

But the teacher wasn't having it. She cut in. "Since your name means 'sky,' we'll call you Sky from now on."

Without flinching, Cielo clapped back. "That's not what my mama named me. My name is Cielo." Full stop.

A sixth-grade mic drop.

My rebel spark ignited. I felt it. Because I knew I was next. I knew I'd have to fight for the silent "H" in *Hugo*. And I did. That day. Every day.

Fast-forward to a few years ago when it came full circle. There I was unexpectedly featured on *The Tonight Show* with Jimmy Fallon and got called up for the "Freestylin' with The Roots" segment. If you've watched the show, you know that Jimmy uses an ad-lib-style approach to gather info on an audience member, and that is turned into a song on the spot by the legendary Roots hip-hop band.

Jimmy asked my name. I said it—Spanish pronunciation, as it is meant to be said. He paused and asked me to repeat it.

In that split second, Cielo's voice echoed in my soul. And I said, clear as ever:

"It's Hugo. Pronounced in Spanish. I'm from Puerto Rico. And my mom *requires* me to say it that way."

Boom.

My name, my story, my flame—broadcast live on national TV. (Jimmy loved it all!)

That moment wasn't just a personal flex. That was a tiny revolution. A reminder that rebellion doesn't always need a bullhorn. It can show up in the *insistence* to be fully, audaciously, unapologetically you.

This book is full of those moments.

Moments when the world tries to shrink you—and you double down instead. Moments when systems break your heart—and you dare to build something better. Moments when you drop the act, stop apologizing, stop waiting for a blueprint—and just start igniting.

Looking back, my life has been one messy masterclass in setting things ablaze without burning out. In challenging dead systems. In leading with a fire sharp enough to ignite others.

And if I've learned anything, it's this: The moments that shape us most don't announce themselves. They creep in during the quiet. They show up in loss. In risk. In the raw, uncurated middle.

You won't always know the fire's been lit—until you feel the heat.

So, let me be clear: This book? It's not here to coddle you. It's here to dare you . . .

Stop stalling.
Stop dimming.
Stop living in draft mode.

This is your final edit. Time to go bold or go home.

It's a field guide for rebel souls. A "day one" friend that is right beside you cheering on the version of you that's tired of being muted. A megaphone for the voice inside you that's ready to roar.

You won't find policies in these pages. No ten-point productivity plan. No soft-focus, latte-fueled affirmations. This isn't self-help. It's *soul work* with teeth and ideas.

And no, it's not a political revolution.

Actually—scratch that.

It *is* a revolution.

A deeply personal one. A full-throttle rebellion against the beige, the boring, the performative. A plea against the slow suffocation of fitting in.

This is your invitation to get SPARKED.

To live like your fire matters. To lead like the world depends on it. To ignite others just by refusing to go dim.

Take the reins of your wild, messy, brilliant life and use it to light something—*anything*—on fire. Do it in a way that makes the world tilt just a little more toward possibility.

Ready? Good.
Because I dare you to see what happens.

Now let's light the damn match.

PART I

# STRIKE THE MATCH

*Where rebellion begins—in identity, purpose, and ignition.*

CHAPTER 1

# THE ORDINARY LIE: COMPLACENCY ISN'T JUST LAZY—IT'S TREASON

"Get busy living or get busy dying."

—*The Shawshank Redemption*

Let me say this loud and clear: Complacency is treason.

Not a mild misstep. Not an unfortunate phase. Treason.

Against your talent.
Against your potential.
Against the world that needs your fire, not your ability to follow a template.

I know this because I lived it.

Rewind the clock to the early 2000s. The world was hungover on dot-com dreams and hiding its anxiety behind boy bands, low-rise jeans, and reality TV. Pop culture was loud. But under the surface? A quiet hum of unease . . . 9/11 had left a psychic bruise. The economy wobbled. Climate whispers became full-throated warnings. And yet, somehow, the narrative stayed polished: *Everything's fine. Keep climbing. Smile for the camera.*

We were told we were chosen, destined for "great power" and, with it, "great responsibility" (right, Spidey?). We were the generation of innovation, of startups, of "disruption." All we had to do was grab an MBA and change the world.

We bought the lie.

I walked straight into it—mid-level pharma job, shiny badge, big energy. I thought I was a rebel stepping into the arena. Turns out I was just another number in the system's spreadsheet.

Strolling onto the corporate ant farm for the first time felt grand, electrifying. Fully stocked gym. On-site dry cleaner. Fancy coffee shop with foam hearts in the lattes. Everything a drone could need.

Except a pulse.
Except a reason.

The job itself? Predictable. Just another meticulously predefined role.

Every task was a checkmark on a spreadsheet—disguised as purpose. We were either too buried in the minutiae to notice the soul death . . . or too coddled by the on-site coffee and dry cleaner to care.

Days blurred into a cycle of repetitive research as we churned through data that sometimes yielded needed insights but almost never the breakthroughs required for true transformation. Frankly, I wasn't sure transformation was even the goal.

Every "win" was an illusion.

Presentations that felt monumental . . . amounted to half a percentage point of progress. Charts. Bullet points. Safe insights. We weren't moving the needle—we were hypnotizing it.

And the culture? At first glance, it wasn't overtly oppressive; in fact, many of the drones were genuinely excited to be contributing, to be part of something *big*.

Management, keen to keep spirits high, frequently rolled out new motivational programs, shiny initiatives, or clever internal campaigns designed to inject a sense of purpose. There were team-building retreats with trust falls and buffet chicken, internal newsletters featuring Ted from accounting's third-place marathon finish. And always, *always* the sacred chant: "It works."

No one dared to ask: *But is it alive?*

Millions kept rolling in, slow and steady into corporate coffers. Why disrupt that? Translation: Don't rock the boat. Cross the t's, dot the i's, hit the quota, rinse, repeat. The unofficial motto, etched deeper than any policy, seemed to be: "We've always done it that way." Processes were carved in stone. Complacency wasn't a bug—it was the entire operating system.

Sound familiar? Or, if you're just starting out, does this blueprint of quiet desperation send shivers down your spine as you begin "adulting"? This wasn't just my experience. This isn't a relic of the past—it's still happening. Across industries. Across titles. Making a mark? Standing out? Innovating? It feels like fighting a ghost. The unspoken agreement: *Don't disrupt. Just deliver.*

You aren't being hired to reinvent the game. You're being hired to fit the slot.

Aggghhhhh!

I felt trapped, drained . . . inspired to make a change. That early job of mine? A crucible. But also a spark. Not a blaze—yet. More like an itch, a crackle, a flicker. A slow, relentless realization: I was not built to blend. Not built to submit. There was something gnawing inside me, demanding more than metrics and milestone decks. I didn't just want to escape—I wanted to destroy and rebuild. I didn't want a different cubicle. I wanted a *different game*.

New ways, fresh ideas—they weren't just wants; they were necessities. While everyone else seemed content to zag, an undeniable urge compelled me to zig. Why? Because the world, as it was, felt drained of color, excitement, and potential. It desperately needed a jolt. It needed a spark! (Are you hearing the swelling music in the background yet?)

A rebel started stirring. Not with a roar—but with a slow, gnawing ache. I wanted more than checklists. More than pats on the head. I didn't just want out—I wanted *different*. I wanted to burn the rulebook and write my own freakin' plays.

And then came *that* movie. *Dead Poets Society*.

A dark theater. Goosebumps. A silent acknowledgment of a truth already stirring within.

It wasn't just a film; it was an unexpected, visceral intervention. Neil Perry, played by the captivating Robert Sean Leonard, dared to speak words that resonated with a primal ache. Thoreau's message hit like thunder:

*"I went to the woods because I wished to live deliberately, to front only the essential facts of life, and see if I could not learn what it had to teach, and not, when I came to die, discover that I had not lived. I wanted to live deep and suck out all the marrow of life."*[1]

Cut to the unconventional Mr. Keating. Robin Williams didn't play a teacher. He played a matchstick. He lit a fire in every kid—and in me. He brought context and direction to the yearning Neil, and all his fictional students felt a profound invitation to seize the day.

And then he said the line that wrecked me: *"No matter what anybody tells you, words and ideas can change the world."*

That movie didn't just resonate—it detonated.

Full, undeniable chills. Instant ignition. This wasn't merely a movie about poetry from days gone by. This was a direct, unfiltered rebel challenge aimed squarely at the audience, a defiant call to arms.

I wasn't just moved.
I was called.

Live deliberately.
Break conformity.
Reject passive existence.
*Carpe diem!*

Mr. Keating wasn't just talking to the characters on screen. In that moment, he was talking directly to me. I walked out of that theater buzzing. Utterly sparked. Ready to seize the day.

---

[1] Thoreau, Henry David. *Walden; or, Life in the Woods*. Ticknor and Fields, 1854.

To live boldly. I wasn't going to let my life blur into grayscale. It had to mean something.

That spark ignited action. It gave me a new perspective on how I needed to show up in the world. I started seeing my mid-level management job through a new lens.

I started messing with the matrix. Sneaking rogue ideas into meetings. Twisting corporate templates into something spicy. Cross-pollinating obsessions. I pitched telenovela scripts to explain medication side effects. (Thanks, Mom, for the early inspiration!) I worked with MTV on a drug company collab. No one asked me to do it. I did it because the old system felt like static.

I was ready to make noise.

That cubicle? It melted. It couldn't contain me anymore. The sheer exuberance and precociousness of my ideas pushed further, truly transforming the role. Ultimately, the cubicle became a distant memory as I began to chase ideas and opportunities that not only propelled the company forward but that also allowed me to explore dreams I'd always had.

Next thing I knew, I was in Greece training pharma reps to use the internet to modernize their old bag of tricks, in Russia presenting at the Kremlin, convincing the Ministry of Health to do an exchange program with mental health patients in the US. I stopped waiting for someone to green-light my dreams. I green-lit *myself*.

Hustle isn't hype. It's preparation.

I didn't just dream. I *backed it up*.

Every "wild" idea? Rooted in more homework, more hustle, more fire than anyone expected. Because to settle would've been a betrayal.

Of my spark.
Of my future.
Of Mr. Keating.

I wasn't chasing promotions. I was chasing *meaning*.

And here's the first truth sparked leaders must embrace: Hustle alone isn't enough. It needs fuel. It needs direction. It needs a spark.

**COMPLACENCY IS A CRIME SCENE**

This is the brutal truth: Passive leadership is a silent betrayal. It's not just boring—it's dangerous. It's a liability in a world that never stops moving. In a world that's on fire, staying neutral is a choice. A dangerous one. If you're not building the future, you're in the way.

The old rules? Obsolete. Yesterday's playbooks are today's shackles. While you're optimizing your inbox, the world is flipping itself inside out. Markets crash and reboot in weeks. Technology rewrites reality daily. (Hello, AI!) One tweet can ignite a movement.

In this relentless current, leaders who merely manage, maintain, or hit "repeat" aren't just falling behind—they're already irrelevant.

The ordinary lie of complacency is treasonous. It's a betrayal of our inherent human capacity for innovation, for progress, for forging a better path. It's an act of surrender to the predictable, a forfeiture of the vibrant future we could actively shape. When we choose to simply maintain, to coast, we aren't just stagnant; we are actively squandering potential—our own, our teams', and the world's. This isn't benign inaction; it's a profound ethical compromise.

The ordinary lie says: *Blend in. Don't question. Don't push*. But every time we accept the lie, we give up the world we *could* be building.

**WHEN NOBODY LEANS IN**

Imagine a world where no one fights for better. A colorless world painted in black, white, and varying shades of gray. What if that gnawing feeling in your gut, that craving for more than compliance, gets smothered? What if the "rinse and repeat" cycle extends beyond the cubicle to define our very existence? Without someone—just a few of us—daring to light a match, to engage with intention, innovation dies. Passion withers. We wouldn't just miss opportunities; we'd flat-out miss entire revolutions, blinded by our own inaction. We'd go numb, spinning in circles of "good enough."

As it is, we frequently allow old ideas to dictate the future. We inadvertently silence the very fresh voices that could guide us forward. We miss the chance for something truly alive, something transformative. And this "rinse and repeat" cycle isn't confined to business; it permeates every facet of life. It traps us in the mundane—personally, professionally, societally. And who truly wants to be a drone? A widget? An afterthought in a world begging for bold strokes? The consequence of disengagement isn't just stagnation; it's a forfeited future.

We must actively lean into changing the world, or else we're simply choosing to inherit one we never truly guided.

What if Steve Jobs never left the garage? What if he hadn't defied the bulky, button-laden phones and the limited capabilities of early mobile tech? What if he hadn't pushed past the "it works" mentality of clunky flip phones and PDAs? (Though I will always have a warm memory of my BlackBerry.) What if he hadn't championed a radical, often insane vision, risking everything, and instead just kept Apple churning out slightly better desktops? What if the iPhone had never been invented? We wouldn't just lack a sleek device in our pocket. We'd lack the entire app economy it spawned—millions of jobs, billions in innovation, entire industries built on connectivity and personalization. We might still be tethered to clunky navigation systems, fax machines, and email accessed only from a desktop. Our social fabric, our access to information, our global interconnectedness—all would look profoundly, primitively different.

What if Netflix kept mailing DVDs? Imagine if Reed Hastings hadn't dared to challenge the behemoth of physical video rentals, pushing for streaming at Netflix when most scoffed? We'd be still driving to Blockbuster, waiting for late fees, and watching entertainment innovation crawl at a glacial pace.

Let's ground this. Time to see how this shows up in real life—on stage, in struggle, in sound.

Extend that to the vibrant tapestry of human expression. What if no one challenged the prevailing artistic norms? No Bad Bunny shattering genre and cultural boundaries? What if Rihanna just remained a pop princess instead of building an empire? No Rolling Stones electrifying stadium rock? Our music would have been stagnant, trapped in a timeless loop. Like me, you might enjoy some classic Charlie Chaplin, but come on . . . sound and color make films so much more exciting, right? Admit it—you watched *Wicked* or *Top Gun: Maverick* or *Avengers: Endgame* or *Barbie* or *Oppenheimer* or whatever . . . and were left breathless. (If you didn't see one of these recent epics, let's talk about your social life in the next book—that's a different kind of sparked journey!) Without change, our films would be devoid of soul, our art an echo, not a roar.

Innovation isn't born from agreement. It's born from tension. From someone saying: "Hell no. We can do better."

Now, let's take it up to the things that truly matter, the very foundations of society. What if no one dared to fight for civil rights, for environmental protection, for gender equality when those battles seemed impossible, even dangerous? What if Rosa Parks hadn't sat where she did on the bus? Or Greta Thunberg hadn't galvanized young people to think about the precarious world they live in? Or Ruth Bader Ginsburg hadn't risen to the highest court in the land, chipping away at centuries of gender-based discrimination? We'd still be living in the shadows of injustices long past, trapped by the suffocating weight of unchallenged history. We would be actively sacrificing the progress we now take for granted.

This isn't a dystopian fantasy; it's the inevitable, slow-motion outcome of the ordinary lie. It's the silent, insidious betrayal that occurs when brilliant minds conform, when passionate individuals opt for comfort over conviction, when leaders choose managing the known over charging into the unknown.

When we allow complacency to reign, we betray not just our own potential but the very future itself. We condemn ourselves and generations to come to a world of monotonous drones, anemic offerings, and countless missed opportunities—a world where the vibrant spark of human ingenuity is extinguished, one un-risked idea at a time.

## THIS IS YOUR SPARKED ERA

This is your moment. It's time to get sparked. To lead on your own terms. To unleash a rebellious leadership mindset that doesn't just show up for life. It crafts it.

This is the essence we're looking to set free: a fierce, personal decision to burn the ordinary, forge your purpose, and ignite change. This book? Your blueprint. Your guide to cultivating that spark, then unleashing a blaze that transforms not just your life but your teams, your organizations, your world.

This isn't about climbing a preset ladder; it's about building your own. A sparked leader doesn't talk big and act safe. Like I did, they zig when others zag. They challenge assumptions. They lead with heart and heat.

If you roam the halls of the corporate world, being a sparked leader might be embracing a visionary role by refusing to accept "that's how we've always done it" as an answer. Picture a senior manager who, instead of implementing another generic cost-cutting measure, champions an innovative, employee-led initiative that boosts morale and productivity, even if it means shaking up traditional departmental silos. They might defy ingrained corporate inertia to push for sustainable practices that genuinely impact the planet rather than just ticking a PR box. Their rebellion isn't loud;

it's systemic, showing up in the policies they rewrite and the teams they empower.

Own your own business? Rebellious leadership looks like the founder who refuses to chase fleeting trends, instead doubling down on a niche, values-driven product or service that truly solves a problem. They might reject the pressure to scale too quickly, prioritizing ethical sourcing and fair wages over rapid, unsustainable growth, even if it means a slower path to profit. Their leadership isn't about imitation; it's about defining their unique value proposition and building a culture around it that radiates authenticity.

In our day-to-day life, we can all be sparked, rejecting the subtle pressures to conform. It's about being the person who commits to being genuinely informed, not just consuming headlines but digging in to truly understand and actively seeking out different perspectives on complex issues.

It's about no longer shrugging off a faraway humanitarian crisis or pretending it doesn't impact you instead finding ways to engage—whether through volunteering time to a local aid organization, advocating for policy change, or simply starting conversations that raise awareness. This is about owning your choices, aligning them with your core purpose, and living a life that leaves a tangible, positive mark on your immediate world by actively striving to be a better global citizen. It's the quiet, consistent defiance of the ordinary, creating extraordinary impact one deliberate choice at a time.

A crucial distinction right now: I'm not talking about leadership confined to a corner office, a fancy nameplate, or a rigid job title. At its core, leadership is the relentless drive to influence, inspire, and move people toward meaningful action—regardless of your role or setting.

A true leader doesn't just manage the existing mess or embody a preconceived notion. They spark movement wherever they are, whenever they are, however they are. They challenge norms, ignite ideas, and empower others to burn brighter. Think of it like a catalyst in a chemical reaction—a great leader accelerates transformation without always needing to claim the spotlight.

Sparked leadership lives in:

- **The student who rallies a campus for a cause.** At the University of Michigan in 2021, a group of students took on a crumbling mental health system—with stories that pierced policy, organizing that forced institutional change, and enough fire to shake the system out of its spreadsheet haze.

  Faced with an undeniable crisis of student well-being and a resource gap that felt like a canyon, these young leaders didn't only lament the problem. They leaned in—hard. They didn't simply sign petitions; they crafted compelling narratives that forced the administration to look beyond raw numbers and see the human cost. They didn't leave it at complaining on social media; they leveraged their digital footprint to ignite a collective will, building a force too significant to ignore.

  Their push didn't just raise awareness—it redirected funding, diversified mental health support, and embedded wellness into campus infrastructure through the Okanagan Charter. This was about tearing down the illusion of passive engagement and forging a profound, lasting impact. It's the kind of brazen leadership that leaves the world—and, in this case, the campus—undeniably better.

Mic drop: They didn't wait for permission. They sparked a system-wide reckoning.

- **The CEO who won't be bound by the expected.** Dan Price wasn't just a business owner. His approach to leadership shrugged off the status quo of executive excess and employee struggle, and along the way, it made a huge impact on how many view their ability to make a difference. In a move that sent shockwaves through the corporate world, Price decided to tweak the compensation model at his company. In fact, he kind of firebombed the model, famously cutting his own million-dollar salary to ensure every single employee at Gravity Payments earned a minimum of $70,000 a year.

  Forget optics. This was rebellion as business strategy—rooted in radical fairness, shared prosperity, and unapologetic human dignity. He refused to accept that a company's success should come at the expense of its lowest-paid workers, proving that a leader can ignite profound change by prioritizing human dignity and economic justice over traditional profit maximization. His actions cultivated a spark on business transformation, challenging the very foundations of how we define value, leadership, and impact in the modern economy.

  Mic drop: Employee morale soared, the company celebrated 100 percent employee retention, and revenue tripled. He proved you can torch the status quo and still come out thriving.

- **The parent who models unwavering integrity in daily choices.** I remember hearing former Olympian Richard George talk about his father's unwavering integrity during a crucial moment in his life. During World War II, when applying to pilot school, his father faced the choice of either concealing a medical condition to ensure his acceptance or being completely truthful, which risked sending him back to the perilous front lines of the infantry. Despite the immense personal cost, George's father chose to disclose his full medical history. And that integrity prevailed when he was accepted to pilot school.

  It wasn't strategy. It was principle—an unflinching commitment to integrity over comfort. Understanding this choice is understanding the heart of a sparked leader. This story takes us beyond mere ethical guidelines; it's about a parent embodying the very essence of truth, proving that true strength lies in an unshakeable commitment to what is right, thereby etching a lasting blueprint for willful, principled leadership in their children.

  Mic drop: That decision didn't just protect his conscience—it modeled sparked leadership for generations.

- **The teammate who lifts others, not just wins.** Have you followed the story of Paige Bueckers, the transcendent basketball star from UConn? While her on-court skills are undeniable and have contributed to the rise in popularity of women's basketball, her true rebellious leadership can be found far beyond the hardwood.

She flipped the script on college athletics, showing that being elite isn't just about stats—it's about purpose. She's aggressively leveraged her massive name, image, and likeness (NIL) platform, not for self-enrichment but to ignite profound community impact. In 2023, she began directing substantial portions of her NIL earnings to combat food insecurity, fund youth sports programs in underserved communities across multiple states, and support initiatives like the Special Olympics and Make-A-Wish Foundation. This wasn't just about charity. It was an intentional statement that made it clear that trailblazers can do more than use their visibility for personal gain; they can forge a profound, tangible community impact, leaving the world a demonstrably better place—one act of radical generosity at a time.

Mic drop: She turned visibility into velocity—and made leadership contagious.

- **The artist who rips open uncomfortable truths through their work.** Make sure you add *Kuleana*, the recent memoir by Sara Kehaulani Goo, to your reading list.

  In *Kuleana*, she doesn't just tell a story—she detonates silence. Her memoir about the battle to reclaim her family's ancestral land in Maui isn't just personal—it's political, spiritual, environmental, and unabashedly confrontational. It's an exposé of the insidious, ongoing legacy of colonialism. Goo's narrative takes us beyond a legal battle into the bare, brutal realities of Indigenous land theft, the compounding trauma, and the relentless bureaucracy that seeks to erase identity and heritage. Her "defiant manifesto" comes alive as she challenges

> readers to confront their own responsibility to Hawai'i, peeling back layers of comfortable ignorance to reveal how historical injustices continue to carve deep wounds in the present, inherently altering the environment and the very way of life for Indigenous peoples.
>
> Mic drop: She doesn't just write about injustice—she dares you to dismantle it.

Are you catching on? It's not about commanding—it's about showing up with purpose and compassion and letting that ripple out. It's about tearing down walls, elevating unheard voices, and responding with empathy. It's about building bridges, not echo chambers.

You see, leadership is about impact, not authority. Whether you're mentoring one person, igniting a global movement, or just being a daily, defiant example of resilience, you're leading.

Another poem referenced in *Dead Poets Society*[2], "O Captain! My Captain"[3] by Walt Whitman, perfectly encapsulates the spirit of challenging the status quo and embracing independent thought that defines a **sparked leader**. While the poem itself mourns a fallen leader after a triumphant journey, Mr. Keating in the film leveraged its raw emotion and stark contrasts to ignite a revolution in his students' minds. He didn't just teach them to analyze it; he used it to make them *feel*, to question prescribed interpretations, and to defy the intellectual conformity of their world. He

---

[2] *Dead Poets Society*. Directed by Peter Weir, performance by Robin Williams, Touchstone Pictures, 1989.

[3] Whitman, W. (1865). O Captain! My Captain! In *Sequel to Drum-Taps*. https://whitmanarchive.org/item/per.00076

pushed them past the literal lines—*"Our fearful trip is done . . . the prize we sought is won . . . But O heart! heart! heart! O the bleeding drops of red, Where on the deck my Captain lies, Fallen cold and dead"*—urging them to find their *own* truth, their *own* voice, even if it meant ripping out pages of conventional wisdom from their textbooks.

This is what you are being called to do as you read this book. (Please don't rip out the pages.) In the movie, Mr. Keating's students stood on their desks to say, *"O Captain! My Captain."* Not because it was polite—but because it was bold.

It was a stand.
A spark.
A declaration that they refused to live small.

This book is your desk.
Stand on it.
Declare it.
Get sparked.

**SPARK PLUGS:**

Throughout this book, our spark plugs will illuminate the path forward. These are not just success stories; they are portraits of individuals who initially grappled with the ordinary lie we've discussed—the seductive pull of complacency, the soul-crushing routine, the pressure to conform. But something within them rebelled. They found their dissident path, proving that the spark isn't inherited; it's ignited through conscious choice and audacious action.

Let's get it started with two such leaders who literally lived the mundane before their rebellious purpose set them free.

## WALT DISNEY: FROM FIRED FOR LACK OF IMAGINATION TO ARCHITECTURAL DREAMER

Before he built an empire of magic and wonder, Walt Disney was intimately familiar with the ordinary lie. His early career was a masterclass in conventional frustration. Imagine being told, as a young man with a boundless imagination, that you *lacked* imagination? That's exactly what happened when Disney was fired from a newspaper for "not being creative enough." He then ventured into animation, but even there, his early studios wrestled with financial collapse, and distribution deals often left him feeling exploited, trapped in the grind of churning out cartoons on someone else's terms.

This wasn't the grand vision. This was the humdrum, the predictable, the "same old, same old'" cycle of merely *making a living* rather than truly *living*. Disney saw the limitations of two-dimensional animation, the fleeting nature of short films, and the transactional reality of Hollywood. But his spark refused to be extinguished. His ultimate rebellion wasn't just to make better cartoons; it was to defy the very idea of entertainment as a passive experience. He envisioned entire worlds—places where stories could be *lived*, where families could *immerse* themselves in magic, where the physical environment itself became part of the narrative. This intractable refusal to accept the boundaries of existing media, this audacious leap beyond conventional animation into architectural dreaming, is what transformed him from a struggling artist into a titan who fundamentally rewrote the rules of imagination and experience.

**SARA BLAKELY:**
**FROM FAX MACHINE GRIND TO HOSIERY DISRUPTOR**

Before she became a self-made billionaire and global icon, Sara Blakely endured the quintessential ordinary lie in her professional life: selling fax machines door to door for seven grueling years. Picture it: the endless cold calls, the rehearsed pitches, the constant rejection, the demoralizing predictability of a job driven purely by quotas and commissions. It was the epitome of "going through the motions," an endless cycle with little room for creativity or genuine impact. She was stuck in a rut that felt devoid of purpose, was just trying to make it through each day.

But beneath the surface of that mundane existence, a rebellious spark flickered. Blakely's true defiance wasn't born in a business school or a startup incubator; it emerged from a deeply personal, relatable frustration: the uncomfortable, unforgiving nature of women's hosiery. She hated pantyhose lines. She was tired of sacrificing comfort for appearance. She refused to accept the industry's unspoken rule that women simply had to endure ill-fitting undergarments. With no background in fashion, retail, or manufacturing, her decision to create a better product was a pure act of rebellion against an entrenched industry that had long dictated what women wore under their clothes. She didn't wait for permission; she took her entire life savings (just $5,000) and threw herself into experimenting, innovating, and doggedly pushing past every "no" she encountered. Blakely's leap from fax machines to Spanx wasn't just about inventing a product; it was about tearing down an old convention, fueled by a personal annoyance that evolved into a global mission to empower women through comfort and confidence.

**GET SPARKED:**

**The Cost of Complacency**

Each chapter in this book challenges you to get sparked—to ignite your own rebellious leadership through actionable prompts. This first exercise is where you confront the ordinary lie head-on, digging deep to expose the hidden costs of inaction and conformity in your own life. Get ready to apply, to question, and to push beyond the ordinary. Your revolution starts now.

**The Prompt:**

Look at an area of your work or personal life where you've been "going through the motions" or sticking to the established script. Be honest with yourself. Where have you quietly accepted the way things are, even when a part of you rebels against it?

**Your Challenge:**

1. List three specific ways this conformity is genuinely costing you. Think beyond just money. Is it costing you:
    - **Lost opportunities?** (Projects you're not pursuing, ideas you're not pitching, experiences you're missing out on.)
    - **Diminished passion?** (That feeling of excitement or joy that has faded from your work or hobbies.)
    - **Feelings of stagnation?** (Feeling stuck, unchallenged, or like you're not growing.)
    - **Compromised values?** (Doing things that don't quite align with what you truly believe in.)
    - **Wasted time or energy?** (Pouring effort into things that don't genuinely matter to you.)

- **Missed connections?** (Not engaging deeply with people or communities that could enrich your life.)
- **A sense of regret or unfulfillment?** (The persistent whisper of "what if?") What's the real, profound price you're paying for accepting the ordinary?

2. Now, jot down one small, defiant thought about how you could reclaim even a tiny piece of that lost potential. This isn't a grand plan; it's a seed of rebellion. It might be a conversation you need to have, a question you need to ask, an email you need to send, or a boundary you need to set.

**Thought to Spark On:**

By exposing the true cost of complacency, you begin to fuel your own spark.

# CHAPTER 2

# DIG LIKE A HERETIC: UNEARTHING THE PURPOSE YOU WERE WARNED ABOUT

"It is not our abilities that show
what we truly are . . . it is our choices."

—*Harry Potter and the Chamber of Secrets*

In the high-octane chaos of modern life, where the gospel of "more, faster, now" blasts at full volume, introspection barely gets a whisper. Purpose? It gets buried under performance reviews and productivity hacks. It can feel less like a journey and more like an archaeological dig. It's not handed to you like a welcome packet. It's buried deep. And digging it out isn't some cute self-help exercise—it's full-on excavation.

But here's the rebellion: You stop digging aimlessly and start excavating what actually matters.

This chapter is your shovel and your spark.

We're not chasing butterflies here. We're mining for fire.

This is where the sparked leader uncovers their heretic purpose—that raw, non-negotiable belief you can't ignore, the one that lights your fuse and dares you to flip tables. It's where vague discomfort turns into righteous fury. It's where ambition stops being polite and becomes dangerous.

Let's be clear: Being a sparked leader doesn't mean torching everything around you. It means getting ferociously honest about what actually matters. It means identifying the thing you'll go to war for. That's your heretic purpose.

This isn't some boilerplate mission statement you slap on a slide deck. This is a battle cry. It's the belief that boils your blood when the world gets it wrong. It's the line in the sand you draw again and again, even when it costs you.

A heretic purpose isn't about rebellion for rebellion's sake. It's about refusing to shrink into easy answers or outdated models. It's about chasing possibility with unrelenting focus—even when that means you're the only one running in that direction.

Because sparked leaders don't wait for permission. They don't beg for consensus. They shift paradigms. They build bonfires out of broken rules.

## BORN TO SWIM AGAINST THE TIDE: MY HERETIC ORIGIN STORY

If we're being totally honest, I think we can agree that "find your purpose" is the bumper sticker of the modern leadership world.

It's been hashtagged, podcasted, vision-boarded, and printed on more mugs than we can count. Yeah, I know—cue the eye roll. Sorry to be piling on but let me make sure you don't miss the truth here. Purpose is sticky for a reason; it refuses to die because it's demanding to be heard. And yeah, it can sound like fluff. Until that ache hits.

That slow-burning question: *What am I actually here for?*

Let's upgrade the ask. What if purpose isn't just about meaning—it's about defiance? About conviction? About choosing to speak truth when silence is safer? That's the level-up. That's heretic purpose.

Mine didn't arrive with trumpets or fireworks. It unfolded like code . . . quietly, steadily. As a first-gen kid who moved from sun-drenched Puerto Rico to the sprawling energy of Chicago, who knew how to translate not just language but culture, expectation, rhythm, my worldview widened quickly. Two worlds collided and rewired my entire sense of identity.

My parents were educators. So, from the jump, I had this gravitational pull toward guidance. Illumination. Legacy. But I wasn't wired to be some Taíno shaman truth-sayer. I was an opinionated, observant kid with commentary for days. I didn't just tell stories . . . I processed the world through them.

My first outlet? A handwritten newsletter called "Vida." (Iconic, right? A little corny too, but sue me—I was a kid!) My brothers didn't read it. My parents didn't read it. I didn't care. It was just for me. I kept writing. That habit—that *need* to express, explain, and connect—never left. My "why" was already in motion.

My influences were everywhere.

I inhaled comic books—Spider-Man, X-Men, Avengers—not just for the action but for the emotional arcs and moral dilemmas. I absorbed how a single panel could convey complex emotion or how a multi-issue arc could build suspense and character development. I read encyclopedias cover to cover, reveling in the systematic uncovering of knowledge, cross-referencing facts, building a mental web of interconnected information.

I toggled between the ridiculously silly worlds of Richie Rich and the profound depths of Shakespeare with equal fascination, understanding that a compelling narrative could come from anywhere. As a latchkey kid, I viewed TV as my ultimate portal. *Looney Tunes* taught me timing and absurdity; sitcoms like *The Cosby Show* (back then) taught me tension, showing me family dynamics and nuanced humor; dramas like *ER* explored complex ethical quandaries and the raw intensity of human stakes. But it was the nightly newscasts that truly fascinated me, teaching me framing.

And watching legendary newsman Tom Brokaw on *NBC Nightly News* one night, I had this *click*. It wasn't the news itself that gripped me; I saw the machine of storytelling at work. Not just what was being said but how it was being shaped. During the intricate setup to a presidential debate, I saw the stage being built, the cameras arrayed, the solemn expressions of the pundits. It was more than just reporting. It was the careful construction of a grand narrative, the myth-building and drama behind the presidential candidates that absolutely crystalized for me how storytelling worked. More than just the facts, it was about framing, about conflict, about creating a world where choices truly mattered.

(Spoiler: Years later, I'd end up working for NBC. With Brokaw. On election night. Full circle magic.)

I soaked it all in indiscriminately. Every show, every character, every narrative became raw material. I wasn't just watching stories. I was absorbing the architecture of them, unconsciously building a mental library of what made people laugh, cry, think, or act.

By high school, I was chasing stories across platforms: journalism, theater, video, whatever I could get my hands on. In college, I launched a bootleg production company using borrowed gear and blind confidence. I was producing live TV with zero safety net. I logged hundreds of hours of trial and error, testing my voice, sharpening my instincts. I learned how to handle a live mic, how to manage an audience, how to pivot when the teleprompter failed. How to edit with a knack for tugging at the heartstrings. It was messy brilliance, and it taught me everything: how to handle havoc, how to earn trust, how to stay human on the mic, how to craft something out of nothing. Somewhere in all that controlled chaos, my purpose began to evolve—from expressive to strategic. I wasn't just telling stories. I was helping others shape theirs—especially those who didn't yet have the words or the platform.

And then, almost by surprise (but, c'mon, we knew where the narrative was pointing, right?), storytelling became my job. By day, I was building growth strategies, mastering brand psychology, and learning how to position ideas so they actually stick. Even in the most corporate corners (yes, the cubicle-filled "pharma years"), I was learning how to connect clarity with emotion, function with feeling. I might have been researching market trends or optimizing product messaging, but beneath it all, I was asking: *What's the story here?*

This wasn't about pitching products; it was about hacking into the human operating system and pulling the emotional levers that actually drive action. This foundation catapulted me into broader, global projects: big brands, small nonprofits, tangible products, abstract ideas, movements. Every time, my heretic purpose showed up: to find the common thread and pull it through with heart and honesty.

This wasn't fluff. It was emotional math. And I realized something: My *deepest* work, the kind that left me vibrating, was always rooted in unlocking stories for the overlooked, the unheard, the underestimated.

Helping a nonprofit leader finally articulate her dream?
Helping a young artist own their message?
Helping a healthcare brand turn data into urgency?

Yes to all of it.

But here's the rebel twist: I also loved working with the big dogs. Household names. Mass-market behemoths. I realized I didn't have to choose between meaning and magnitude. I could bridge both. I *wanted* to bridge both. Because it's not about scale. It's about truth.

These days, I don't just tell stories. I architect experiences that shake people. I write. I direct. I teach. I build. I cook. (Seriously, a good meal is a masterclass in storytelling.)

My heretic purpose is to connect big, bold ideas to deeply human truths. To bring soul to strategy. To put heartbeat in the pitch. To spark things that actually matter.

Because basic purpose is fine. But heretic purpose? That's the spark that sets the whole system on fire.

Pause.

Now let's talk about the voice under the noise—the one you've been taught to ignore.

## THE GUT-PUNCH DECISION: CHOOSING MEANING OVER MEDIOCRITY

This isn't just about my journey. The larger truth is this: Purpose isn't a personality trait. It's a *decision*. A line you choose to draw. A mirror you refuse to look away from.

This is the very heart of your heretic purpose: the moment you stop playing by the rules simply because they exist. It's the moment you decide *I'm not here to* fit *the mold; I'm here to* melt *it*.

It's the resolution not to compete within boundaries but to challenge and redefine the boundaries themselves. It's what happens when you stop chasing consensus and start living by unwavering conviction.

A heretic purpose doesn't just whisper meaning into your work—it rewires your leadership. Remember, it's not about being rebellious for rebellion's sake. There's nothing chaotic or reckless in a sparked leader. Instead, you're just unshakably, brazenly real. You're crystal clear.

Clear about what matters.

Clear about who you serve.

Clear about what you're willing to push against—even if it makes things uncomfortable. You don't just want to make a dent. You want to flip the whole blueprint.

You aren't merely trying to occupy space in the market or grab the spotlight; you're trying to shift paradigms, provoke thought, spark conversation, and, ultimately, redefine the very game itself.

Think of Oprah Winfrey. Her rebellion wasn't against a product or a political system but against the narrow definitions of daytime television, media ownership, and what a Black woman from a marginalized background could achieve. She didn't just host a talk show; she consciously redefined the medium, building an empire rooted in authenticity, empathy, and empowerment. Her willfulness wasn't loud or destructive; it was the muted, unyielding power of living her heretic purpose: to elevate, to connect, to inspire self-improvement. She rewrote the rules of influence and media engagement. Baller!

In the same way, I think of the kid from suburban Illinois with Ghanaian parents, trained as an engineer and architect, who refused to accept that luxury belonged only to the gatekeepers of Paris. Virgil Abloh didn't just design clothes; he hacked the entire fashion system. Through Off-White and his work at Louis Vuitton, he dismantled the walls between streetwear and haute couture, between culture and commerce, between the runway and the block. His heretic purpose wasn't to mimic the establishment but to remix it, to prove that creativity could be both subversive and accessible. Abloh turned collaboration into rebellion, treating design as a language of inclusion. His runway wasn't about fabric; it was about possibility. He didn't just change fashion; he changed who got to dream within it. (Raising my hand high here! I'm one of those dreamers!)

Rosalind Franklin was another kind of heretic—the quiet, razor-sharp scientist whose rebellion lived in her precision. In the 1950s, while the scientific world was still gatekept by male egos, she captured the X-ray diffraction image that revealed DNA's double helix structure, the literal blueprint of life. Her colleagues, Watson and Crick, famously ran with her data and claimed the glory, but Franklin's heretic purpose wasn't fame. It was truth. Her refusal to play the politics of recognition, her insistence on the integrity of her work, became its own form of defiance. She didn't shout to be seen; she let the science speak. And in doing so, she redefined what it means to lead with intellectual courage in a system built to overlook you.

I also think of Timnit Gebru who lit her match inside the algorithm. As a pioneering computer scientist and one of the first Black women in her field to lead ethical AI research at Google, she dared to question the unchecked power of Big Tech from the inside. Her heretic purpose? To expose how bias gets baked into code and how the systems we call "neutral" often replicate the same old injustices at scale. When she was forced out for co-authoring a paper that critiqued the very technology she was helping to build, it became clear: Her rebellion wasn't just technical—it was moral. Gebru didn't retreat. She doubled down, founding the Distributed AI Research (DAIR) Institute to reimagine what responsible innovation could look like when centered on justice and inclusion. In a world obsessed with optimization, she chose integrity. That's sparked leadership.

To be honest, I dream of earning my place in this wild lineage of heretics—the ones who refused to color inside the lines and instead redrew the damn canvas. The ones who turned doubt into movement and disruption into ministry. They weren't trying to be famous. They were trying to be free. And that's the spark I'm chasing too.

The level of purpose we've been exploring demands a different kind of leadership—one rooted in meaning, not metrics. Let's talk about how that looks like in practice:

- **Flip the Script:** Time to stop drinking the Kool-Aid. Start interrogating every "best practice" like it's on trial.

  This isn't just a philosophical stance; it's a strategic imperative. It means actively questioning the foundational "truths" of your field—those unspoken rules or conventional wisdoms everyone accepts.

  For example, in a sales-driven industry, the assumption might be "the loudest voice wins." A sparked leader might challenge that by proving that deep listening and tailored solutions build stronger, more sustainable client relationships. You ask: *Why is it done this way? Who really benefits? Who might be excluded by this default setting?*

  Sparked leaders aren't cynics. They're system critics. They take inherited wisdom and stress-test the hell out of it. They rigorously test it, prod at its weaknesses, and, if necessary, dismantle it, arriving at wisdom with genuine meaning and real-world applicability. If it fails? They rebuild. Not for the sake of rebellion—but for the sake of relevance and justice.

- **Blow Up the Playing Field:** Why compete in a broken game when you could invent your own?

  Forget grabbing a slice of the pie. Being led by a heretic purpose drives you to bake a new, entirely different pie. This isn't about incremental innovation; it's about radical reimagining. Think of how Airbnb didn't just compete with hotels; they rewrote hospitality. Or how

Tesla didn't just make a faster car; they made an electric vehicle that fundamentally reshaped the perception of automotive power and sustainability. It's about inventing categories, setting new benchmarks, and rendering old models obsolete, not through tiny improvements but by bold, systemic shifts.

Sparked leaders see the cracks in the system and say, "What if we just blow it up and start fresh?" The phrase "we've always done it that way" is like kryptonite—a signal that an unchallenged assumption is ripe for disruption.

- **Stand for Something . . . Don't Just Sell Something:** Beliefs build tribes. Features build boredom.

  While benefits (what your product or service *does*) are, of course, important, a sparked leader with a heretic purpose anchors themselves and their organization to deeply held beliefs and core convictions (what your product or service *stands for*). All their offerings then flow naturally from this mission. This isn't just about selling a product or service; it's about inviting people to join a movement, to align with a shared worldview.

  When you buy a brand because you believe in its values, you become an advocate, not just a customer. This creates a far more powerful and resilient connection than any feature-benefit list ever could. It fosters a community built on shared principles where loyalty transcends mere utility.

  People don't join movements because of discounts. They join because you echo something they believe deep in their bones. You're not just selling. You're inviting people to *belong*.

**HERETIC BUSINESSES THAT IMPLEMENTED THE PLAYBOOK**

The following industries were rocked when their sparked leaders chose to redefine business by leaning into heretic purposes:

- **Ben & Jerry's:** More than just ice cream, their purpose is intertwined with social justice. From fair trade ingredients to advocating for marriage equality and racial justice, their flavors often serve as a vehicle for their progressive politics. When you buy their ice cream, you're also investing in their mission for a more equitable world.
- **Liquid Death:** In a market dominated by bland, "healthy" hydration, Liquid Death emerged with a punk-rock, anti-marketing ethos. Their purpose? To "murder your thirst" and, more profoundly, to challenge the absurdity of traditional beverage advertising while promoting sustainable packaging. They don't sell hydration—they sell middle fingers to plastic bottles and performative wellness culture. And it works.
- **Pedagogy of the Oppressed:** Paulo Freire wasn't just an educator; he was a revolutionary with a chalkboard. His landmark work, *Pedagogy of the Oppressed*, flipped the entire educational paradigm by insisting that learning is not about memorization but liberation. He challenged the "banking model" of education—where teachers deposit information into passive students—and replaced it with a radical belief: that students are co-creators of knowledge. He didn't just teach. He rewired the very purpose of education itself.

- **Dove's "Real Beauty" Campaign:** In an industry obsessed with unattainable perfection, Dove dared to challenge the prevailing beauty standards. Their purpose shifted from simply selling soap to promoting self-esteem and celebrating authentic beauty in all its forms. This conviction-driven campaign didn't just boost sales; it ignited a global conversation and fundamentally altered the advertising landscape for personal care products.

These companies were guided by leaders who didn't play nice. They played real. And they built brands people would *bleed* for.

Am I making the point? The challenge isn't to be negative or adversarial for its own sake. It's about being strategic, often compassionate, with a willingness to ruffle feathers if that's what it takes to make things genuinely better. It's about understanding that true progress rarely emerges from placid consensus. It often springs from the friction created when comfortable assumptions are challenged, when inconvenient truths are brought to light, and when the status quo is firmly yet intentionally prodded.

Sparked leaders guided by a heretic purpose aren't trying to be polarizing just to grab headlines. (Many of us prefer to avoid the headlines altogether.) Instead, they refuse to water down meaning or value to appease the widest possible audience. Their messaging might not initially resonate with everyone; it's designed to cut through the noise for those who are truly listening. But to *those who matter most*, it will be unforgettable, even magnetic. And that's how they ignite grassroots passion that sparks bit by bit, reaching the masses through genuine resonance. That's how movements start. That's how brand loyalty turns into belief.

These are the disruptors, the paradigm shifters, the catalysts for genuine change. The ones who understand that leading with purpose means making bold, often uncomfortable choices. It means being willing to lose the crowd in order to spark a community. And it means never settling for relevance when you're called to be revolutionary.

Let's pause here to untangle something that trips up a lot of people, especially rebel-hearted ones.

Passion. Purpose. Calling.

They sound interchangeable, but they aren't. Passion fuels energy—it gets you out of bed with excitement. Purpose fuels direction—it gives your spark somewhere to go. And calling? Calling fuels courage. It's what steadies you when the applause stops and the terrain gets rough. Passion can be loud, even chaotic. Purpose narrows the beam. But calling? Calling keeps you walking when nobody else sees the path.

**REFLECTION BREAK: BEFORE THE MOVEMENT**

Before we go deeper, let's be brutally clear: Your heretic purpose? It won't always be met with applause. It might shake the ground you stand on. It might cost you comfort, friendships, even your sense of belonging—*before* it gifts you focus.

And that's not just normal. It's necessary.

I've lived it.

Like the moment I ran headfirst into one of the most seductive versions of the ordinary lie, the one dressed up as "play the game and you'll be rewarded."

I was eighteen months into my gig at the pharmaceutical company. Grinding, winning, and playing the long game. I was delivering results. Big ones. My team was thriving, my campaigns were landing, and the PR headlines were glowing. I did what they told me success required: make the higher-ups look good, play the game, keep the good of the company front and center, and—eventually—my moment would come.

And then it did. Kind of.

After returning from that high-profile marketing exchange in Russia—a capstone to a year of wins—I was pulled into a meeting. The tone was celebratory. I was being promoted. Finally. Recognition. A breakthrough.

Except . . .

Right as they handed me the title, they also handed it to everyone else at my level. "To be fair," they said. "To avoid singling you out."

Translation? You broke the mold, so we changed the rules. We raised the ceiling just to keep you in the same room.

That's how the ordinary lie sustains itself—it moves the goalpost when you get too close to the truth. When you shine too brightly, it dims the whole room. Because your growth threatens its control.

That moment didn't break me though. It ignited me.

It was the clearest invitation I'd ever received:
To stop playing by rules that weren't designed for me to win.
To stop trading in my spark for someone else's scoreboard.
To stop mistaking proximity for power.

Because the fact is that purpose isn't polite. It's disruptive. But disruption doesn't mean destruction.

When your fire is grounded in service, not ego, your spark doesn't need to incinerate everything in its path. It lights the way forward.

So let this sink in: A spark doesn't have to scorch to leave a mark.

The Taíno people of Puerto Rico, my ancestral roots, have a saying: "The river does not try to be the sea. It flows its own path."

Flow like that.

Bold. Clear. Unapologetic.

Be your own river. And trust that your movement starts there.

**WHEN YOUR HERETIC PURPOSE IGNITES A MOVEMENT**

So, when does unearthing and embracing this heretic purpose really take off? When does your spark become a wildfire?

- **When you bring your audience something that feels real, raw, human.** Think about the explosion of craft breweries or independent coffee shops that captivated consumers fed up with mass-produced, one-size-fits-all options. In a world saturated with generic promises and endless noise, people are yearning for authenticity, for a genuine connection. If your industry has lost its way, if its offerings feel stale and disingenuous, getting sparked with a heretic purpose means becoming a beacon for those desperate for something true, something that aligns with their deeper values.

- **When your category is comatose and you show up with a cattle prod.** If innovation has slowed to a crawl, if everyone's playing it safe, adhering to the same tired formulas, that's precisely when a sparked leader with a heretic purpose can disrupt the entire ecosystem. It's about recognizing the silent desperation of a market segment that's begging for a jolt, a fresh perspective, a challenge to its very foundations. Think of how Casper shook up the mattress industry, not just by selling beds online but by questioning the entire mattress buying experience itself.
- **When your work taps into something bigger than you.** Your purpose gains incredible leverage when it connects to a larger, ongoing societal shift, a pressing ethical question, or a deeply felt cultural need. If you can genuinely align your work with something bigger than just profit or personal gain—like fighting climate change, advocating for social equity, or championing mental well-being—your impact transcends commerce or mere advocacy. You become an undeniable part of a larger, more urgent conversation, drawing energy and support from those who share your conviction. You're not just selling; you're showing up.
- **When you attract believers, not buyers.** A heretic purpose isn't about transactions; it cultivates fierce, unshakeable loyalty. It transforms consumers into passionate advocates, employees into tireless missionaries, and casual observers into engaged, passionate participants. People don't just use your product. They wear your values. They tell your story like it's their own. Because

it *is*. They are the ones who will stand by you, defend you, and spread your message organically because your purpose resonates with their own deepest values.

A sparked leader isn't motivated by trying to fit in. Quite the opposite—they want to wake people up. They lead with a potent blend of compassion and fierce conviction, with an almost irresistible interest that entices others to really go there—to dig deeper, to question more profoundly, to engage with their whole selves. They go beyond just marketing a product or sharing a cause.

Here's that movement we've been talking about. (Cue the arena anthem in the background!) They get that true leadership isn't just about the path you walk but the new pathways you forge for others to follow.

Now it's your turn.

Stop waiting for signs.
Start digging.

And if you hit something that scares you a little?
You're probably on the right path.

Let's go.

**SPARK PLUG:**
**Yvon Chouinard and the Ultimate Rebellion**
When it comes to unearthing a heretic purpose and letting it dictate every fiber of an enterprise, few leaders embody this more sincerely than Yvon Chouinard, the sparked visionary founder of Patagonia. His journey didn't begin in a boardroom but on the jagged rock faces he loved to climb. This deeply personal passion for wild places fused with an unrelenting commitment

to quality and, crucially, to the planet, made him a "heretic" in consumerism long before environmentalism was mainstream.

Chouinard's purpose was the ultimate rebellion: to build the best products, cause no unnecessary harm, and use business to protect nature. This wasn't a marketing tagline; it was a deeply held conviction that permeated every decision. When faced with the realization that his company's core climbing equipment was damaging rock, he redesigned it, even if it meant disrupting his own successful product line. When fast fashion took hold, Patagonia launched their "Don't Buy This Jacket" campaign, actively urging customers to consume less, repair more, and think critically—an intractable act of anti-consumerism in a growth-obsessed industry. He consistently chose environmental stewardship over profit maximization, from pioneering recycled materials to donating 1 percent of sales to environmental causes. More recently, he famously transferred ownership of Patagonia to a trust and nonprofit, ensuring all future profits would be used to fight climate change.

Chouinard didn't just build a brand. He detonated a myth: that you can't grow a business while serving a higher purpose. His heretic purpose became Patagonia's pulse, defying capitalism's greed gospel and replacing it with a living commitment to purpose. That's not just rebellion. That's revolution stitched into every seam.

**GET SPARKED:**

**The Heretic's Core**

Your heretic purpose isn't something you passively stumble upon; it's actively unearthed by digging into what truly agitates you, what injustice you refuse to accept, what broken system you're compelled to mend.

This exercise is designed to strip away the "shoulds" and the "can'ts" and get to the raw core of your defiant conviction.

**The Prompt:**
Imagine for a moment that you possess an unlimited budget and a guarantee of success. The usual constraints of resources, time, and feasibility simply vanish. With these superpowers at your disposal, what single problem, injustice, or inefficiency in the world—or within your industry or organization—would you dedicate your entire life to solving? What is that one thing that infuriates you so deeply, so consistently, that you literally *can't not* think about it? This raw, almost obsessive emotion is not a distraction; it's a potent, pure source of your heretic purpose.

**Your Challenge:**

1. **Articulate this "unsolvable" problem in one bold, precise sentence.** Make it punchy. Make it undeniable.
2. **List three compelling reasons why solving this problem would mean the world to you.** These aren't just logical points; they're the emotional, visceral connections that fuel your deepest drive. What personal values would it fulfill? What historical wrongs would it right? What kind of future would it unlock for others or for the world?

**Thought to Spark On:**
This exercise isn't about grandiosity; it's about honing your thinking. It's about peeling back layers of practicality to reveal the defiant, conviction-driven core of your leadership. What's the problem only *you* are truly compelled to solve?

# CHAPTER 3

# THE REBEL LENS: CULTIVATING A RADICAL SKEPTICISM OF THE STATUS QUO

"There is no spoon."

—*The Matrix*

Welcome to the real world.

Remember when *The Matrix* detonated into pop culture? It wasn't just a film; it was a cinematic mic drop, a philosophical gauntlet, a full-blown mindquake. It didn't just flex slow-mo bullets and black leather—it cracked open the illusion of normal. It posed a nuclear-grade question: *What if everything you believe is real is actually a carefully coded lie?* It asked us to question the very fabric of our reality, prompting a global conversation about perception, control, and the hidden forces that might be shaping our lives.

In the middle of the mayhem, a quiet line lands like a thunderclap: "There is no spoon."

At first glance, it's just cryptic movie dialogue. But look deeper—it's a philosophical Molotov cocktail hurled straight at convention. It's a stubborn call to shatter limitations you didn't even know you had. It's a battle cry for rebel leaders who refuse to accept reality as handed down.

Welcome to the rebel lens: not a tool, not a trick—a whole new way of seeing.

## FROM PURPOSE TO PERCEPTION

It's not enough to know what you stand for. You've got to see what others don't. You must train your eyes to cut through clutter, pierce through illusion, and read between the lines of reality. That means spotting the invisible tethers of broken systems, outdated assumptions, and lazy thinking that most people walk past every day.

This chapter is about seeing unbridled possibility amidst what others deem insurmountable obstacles. It's about transforming your weariness of the prevailing order into a powerful, strategic, and profoundly liberating advantage.

This is not about becoming jaded. This is not about intellectual snobbery or armchair rebellion. It's about radical skepticism—a disciplined refusal to accept reality as is and the audacity to imagine it as it could be. Because when you look through a rebel lens, you don't just see problems; you see opportunities masquerading as obstacles. You don't just see limits; you see a boundless canvas for reinvention, a chance to sculpt a reality far more vibrant and effective. This is where you move from just observing the world to actively *crafting* it.

High-potential leaders who consistently see possibility amidst obstacles and relentlessly question limiting assumptions must hone a powerful mix of practical cognitive, interpersonal, and strategic skills. These aren't abstract academic theories; they're muscles you can build, tools you can wield, to challenge the very fabric of the ordinary and unlock an extraordinary future.

## THROUGH A REBEL'S EYES, THE WORLD REBUILDS ITSELF

Radical skepticism is about asking the questions no one dares to. It's interrogating the "obvious," flipping the "normal," and disrupting the unquestioned. It's training your mind to not only spot cracks in the system—but to see *through* them. To sketch bold alternatives in the margins where others only see dead ends.

And it's learnable. It's a skill set. A mindset. A muscle group.

Sparked leaders see patterns in the chaos, feel tension in the silence, and ask "Why?" when everyone else is nodding along. They possess a tool kit of essential rebel skills—each one a sharp edge for cutting through the noise.

Let's hone that tool kit. The following are seven superpowers of the rebel lens. Each one of these skill sets fuels your ability to decode, disrupt, and reimagine. Together, they turn your rebel lens from a curiosity into a weapon of reinvention.

**1. Systems Thinking – Seeing the Matrix:** This is your macro vision, the ability to zoom out and grasp the interconnected dance of people, power, process, and policy. It's like seeing the entire forest, not just individual trees. It's how you see the roots under the weeds. You're not just looking at isolated problems; you're seeing patterns, how things feed into each other, and all the unexpected side effects. It's understanding that if you tweak one thing over here, it's going to ripple across the whole system.

You don't just fix problems—you dissect *why* they exist.

**Practical use:**

- **Finding the real reasons behind problems:** You don't just see a surface-level issue; you dig into *why* it's happening within the bigger picture. For example, if a company's struggling to keep good people, most might just look at why folks are leaving. But a systems thinker would connect the dots: Are training programs lacking? Is management style an issue? What about promotion opportunities, pay, or even local community support?
- **Pinpointing where to make the biggest difference:** Once you truly get the system, you can find small, powerful points where a targeted change can create massive positive shifts in how things are done, what rules are followed, or what the culture feels like. This isn't about slapping a band-aid on symptoms; it's about actually fixing the core operating system.

**Build it through:**

- **Learning from diverse real-world stories:** Study what made other companies or movements succeed or fail, even if they're totally different from yours. How did city planning affect health? How did a factory shift change global supply chains?
- **Drawing out connections:** Literally sketch out how different parts of a problem or situation influence each other. Seeing it visually will help you uncover hidden forces at play.
- **Broadening your reading list:** Don't just stick to your industry's books. Dive into sociology, psychology,

history, even environmental science. Every field offers a fresh way to understand complex systems.

Let's shift lenses. Because seeing clearly starts with seeing differently.

**2. Strategic Questioning – Start a Mental Riot:**
You're not here to ask polite questions. You're here to probe, flip, provoke—to uncover blind spots and torch assumptions with "What if?", "Why not?", and "Who benefits from this staying broken?" It's about choosing curiosity over certainty, actively dismantling the unwritten rules that usually guide your thinking.

**Practical use:**

- **Flipping the script in conversations:** In important discussions, ask, "What if the opposite were true? Whose voice isn't being heard here?" "If everyone agrees on 'X,' what if 'not X' was the answer?" "Who's missing from the conversation?" "Whose experience are we overlooking?" These questions force everyone to rethink ingrained beliefs.
- **Turning problems into launchpads:** Instead of asking, "How do we fix this bug?", ask, "How might this 'bug' actually point to a new feature we never considered or a deeper need our users have?"
- **Digging into the "why" behind the "what":** Before you jump to solutions, always ask *why* something needs to be done at all or *why* it has to be done in a specific way. You'll be surprised how often there's no good answer.

**Build it through:**

- **Practicing "the 5 Whys":** For any problem or assumption, keep asking "why" at least five times to drill down to its true root. You'll often find surprisingly illogical or outdated origins for "we've always done it that way."
- **Engaging in Socratic questioning:** Lead discussions in which you gently guide others to explore their own beliefs and reasoning, helping *them* discover new insights instead of just telling them.
- **Regular self-reflection:** Keep a journal or set aside time to ask yourself: *What did I assume today that turned out not to be true?* or *What critical question did I* not *ask that might have changed the outcome?*

**3. Cognitive Flexibility – Pivot Like a Ninja:**

The world shifts. Algorithms evolve. Culture flips. The rebel mind doesn't break under that pressure—it bends, adapts, flourishes. It's the mental nimbleness to comfortably hold seemingly conflicting ideas and to thrive in uncertainty.

Flexibility is your mental jiu-jitsu.

**Practical use:**

- **Navigating choppy waters without freezing up:** When unexpected challenges hit, a cognitively flexible leader can quickly rethink, adjust plans, and explore new paths instead of getting stuck or clinging to old, failing strategies.
- **Planning for multiple futures:** Instead of betting everything on a single "Plan A," actively think through "Plan B," "Plan C," and even "Plan Z." This prepares you

for a range of possibilities, making you more resilient in a constantly changing world.

- **Embracing complex ideas:** It's important to understand that seemingly opposite ideas (like radical innovation *and* careful ethics) aren't always in conflict. In fact, they can often exist together and even make each other stronger.

**Build it through:**

- **Listening beyond your lane:** Pop in the earbuds and deliberately step outside your bubble. Try a sports podcast to rethink strategy and teamwork. Sit with a money guru that might challenge your definition of "enough." Drop into a faith convo to understand where conviction and devotion are forged. Growth happens when you let unfamiliar voices stretch how you think.
- **Role-playing and simulations with your team:** Actively put yourselves in the shoes of competitors, critics, or even a customer with a very different background. This forces you to think beyond your usual perspective.
- **Actively seeking out diverse viewpoints:** Make an effort to connect with people who see the world fundamentally differently than you do. Your goal isn't to argue but to genuinely understand their mental framework.

**4. Deep Listening – Tune into the Frequency Beneath Words:** Rebels don't just listen—they *detect*. They hear what's unsaid. They read the silence. They feel what's hiding behind the smile. It's tuning into the subtle energy of human interactions and the hidden dynamics of any system.

**Practical use:**

- **Sensing the unspoken vibe:** You pick up on the hidden cultural tensions, muted anxieties, or unexpressed hopes within your team or community. This goes way beyond surveys; it's about feeling the actual *mood* of the room or the organization.
- **Uncovering the real source of problems:** Often, what people *say* is the problem isn't the whole story. Deep listening helps you find the underlying frustrations, fears, or misalignments that are truly driving conflict or disengagement.
- **Building real trust and connection:** When people feel genuinely heard—not just waited out—it builds a strong foundation for honest conversation and true collaboration, which is crucial for any disruptive effort.

**Build it through:**

- **Practicing silence in conversations:** Seriously, resist the urge to jump in, fill awkward pauses, or plan your next witty response. Just listen. *Really* listen. Let them finish.
- **Exploring frameworks like Nonviolent Communication (NVC)[4] or restorative listening circles:** These offer structured ways to train your ear to listen for deeper needs, feelings, and underlying motivations.
- **Mindful observation in your daily life:** Pay attention to body language, shifts in tone, and the way groups interact in casual settings, not just formal meetings. What's the unspoken story here?

---

[4] Rosenberg, M. B. (2015). *Nonviolent Communication: A Language of Life* (3rd ed.). Encinitas, CA: PuddleDancer Press.

**5. Values-Based Decision Making – Lead with a Spine:**
When the data is murky and the map is torn, your values are your compass. Rebels make unpopular decisions with resolute clarity because their "why" is tattooed on their bones. This means grounding your leadership firmly in your core principles, giving you unwavering integrity even when things are unclear or messy.

**Practical use:**

- **Making tough calls when numbers aren't enough:** When you face a choice where there's no clear "best" quantitative answer, your values step in as the ethical framework that guides your decision.
- **Leading big changes without losing trust:** When you communicate decisions, even unpopular ones, through the clear lens of your values, people understand *why* you made them. This builds deep respect and long-term loyalty, even if they don't fully agree.
- **Creating stability in chaos:** In times of uncertainty or disruption, a clear, shared set of values provides a steady foundation for you and your team to fall back on.

**Build it through:**

- **Getting crystal clear on your personal and organizational values:** What truly matters to you? What does your team or organization stand for? Write them down, talk about them, refer to them constantly.
- **Using ethical frameworks (like stakeholder analysis or long-term impact mapping[5]):** Before making a big

[5] Adzic, G. (2012). *Impact mapping: Making a big impact with software products and projects*. MindMup Press.

decision, consciously consider its impact on everyone involved and its ethical implications down the road, not just the immediate benefits.

- **Seeking out diverse ethical perspectives:** Dive into philosophy, different religious texts, or even fiction that explores complex moral dilemmas. This broadens your ethical reasoning and helps you navigate nuance.

**6. Pattern Recognition – Decode the Static:**

You see what others miss—trends before they trend, risks before they detonate, and connections no one else thought to make. This is the advanced skill of looking at seemingly disparate information and interpreting it in meaningful, insightful ways. It's seeing the hidden connections that others miss, spotting the emerging story before it becomes obvious to everyone else.

**Practical use:**

- **Catching early warnings of change:** You develop an almost uncanny ability to spot tiny signals that might foreshadow massive shifts in how people behave, what new technologies are on the rise, or what's happening in society. This lets you pivot *before* the storm hits, not react to it.
- **Finding surprising links between unrelated things:** You might see how a change in global politics influences local buying habits or how a breakthrough in one scientific field could completely revolutionize another. You're always looking for the unexpected bridge.
- **Turning raw data into compelling stories:** You can take complex information and transform it into insights that

not only make sense but also resonate emotionally and compel action—a crucial skill for any true storyteller.

**Build it through:**

- **Studying historical disruptions:** Immerse yourself in the stories of past revolutions and innovations. What were the early signs? Who saw them, and who missed them?
- **Actively synthesizing diverse information:** Regularly pull together content from all sorts of sources—articles, podcasts, casual conversations, detailed reports—and challenge yourself to find the big-picture patterns or emerging themes.
- **Cultivating endless curiosity:** Continuously ask "why" things are the way they are. Spend time observing human behavior in public, read widely outside your comfort zone, and always be looking for the unexpected.

**7. Observational Intelligence – Master the Micro-Move:**
This is Jedi-level perception. It's reading the room before anyone speaks, sensing a fracture in culture, or catching the buried emotion under someone's "I'm fine." This is a sharpened, almost intuitive awareness of everything around you: context, body language, subtle system cues, and tiny "micro-signals" that most people completely overlook.

**Practical use:**

- **Instantly understanding group dynamics:** You can walk into a meeting and quickly pick up on power struggles, hidden agendas, or unseen barriers that are blocking progress. This helps you tailor your approach and address real resistance.

- **Spotting disconnects in culture:** You notice when an organization's stated values no longer line up with what people are actually doing or when morale is eroding beneath the surface.
- **Grasping customer pain points beyond direct feedback:** Instead of just asking for feedback, you observe *how* people interact with your product or service, noticing their frustrations, their workarounds, or where they get stuck.

**Build it through:**

- **Getting out of the office:** Do "field visits," observe customers in their natural environment (ethnographic observation), or even shadow frontline workers. This puts you directly in the context you need to understand.
- **Mindful reflection:** Take reflective walks or keep a journal where you deliberately notice details—sounds, smells, subtle gestures, patterns of interaction—and then spend time thinking about what they might mean.
- **Practicing genuine presence:** Make an effort to be fully present in conversations and interactions, not distracted by your phone or your own thoughts. This heightened focus allows you to pick up on those subtle but crucial cues.

## MORE THAN SKILLS—IT'S REWIRING YOUR DEFAULT

This isn't a list to check off. It's a neural revolution.

Curiosity over control. Precision over performance. Insight over impulse.

This isn't a passive assimilation of knowledge. It's an active, relentless re-focusing of your mind, a purposeful commitment to seeing through a brand-new set of lenses. It's fueled by a voracious appetite for active learning—not just consuming information but truly engaging with it. It means diving headfirst into robust debates, welcoming dissenting opinions, and constantly considering the world around you from every conceivable angle.

As Malcolm Gladwell explored in *Blink*, true expertise isn't always about conscious, systematic processing.[6] Sometimes, the most profound insights come from "thin-slicing"—rapid cognition, where years of experience and honed intuition allow you to make lightning-fast, accurate judgments. Sparked leaders aren't always systematically thinking through each of these skill sets in a linear fashion. Instead, they lean into lives of consequence, constantly and almost instinctively leveraging these concepts in every decision they make and action they take.

You don't wield these skills once and move on—you wear them like armor, sharpen them like blades. They become your operating system.

The rebel lens doesn't wait for permission—it scans, questions, remakes.

**REAL-WORLD FIRESTARTERS**

The most impactful leaders don't just stumble into purpose. They actively cultivate it with radical skepticism. This allows

[6] Gladwell, M. (2005). *Blink: The Power of Thinking Without Thinking*. Little, Brown and Company.

them to spot what others completely miss, challenge what everyone else accepts, and ignite change where most see only brick walls. Their rebel lens doesn't just point out problems; it reveals the incredible possibilities hidden right inside those obstacles.

Here are three heretics. Three realities. One rebellious lens that changed everything.

### CRISTINA JIMÉNEZ MORETA: UNWAVERING ADVOCATE FOR IMMIGRANT YOUTH

Cristina Jiménez Moreta, a celebrated immigrant rights activist and co-founder of United We Dream, epitomizes the power of the rebel lens in a context fraught with systemic injustice and human vulnerability. Having emmigrated from Ecuador to the US as a child without documents, she fights tirelessly for the rights and dignity of undocumented youth, challenging a system that often leaves them in the shadows, living with constant fear.

Jiménez Moreta's brilliance lies in her acute observational intelligence and her profound understanding of systems thinking. She doesn't just see individuals in precarious situations; she recognizes how intersecting disadvantages (immigration status, race, class, and age) create complex, often paralyzing cycles of exclusion and exploitation for young people. She keenly observes how institutions—from immigration enforcement to educational access and even the legislative process—uphold structural inequalities designed to keep undocumented communities disempowered. She sees the vast gap between America's stated values of opportunity and the actual, dehumanizing reality faced by millions. Rather than accepting this status quo, she disrupts these norms at their root, leading a movement that empowers undocumented youth themselves to become vocal advocates. Through strategic organizing, powerful storytelling, and bold direct action, United We Dream moves Deferred Action for Childhood Arrivals (DACA) from an abstract concept to a tangible policy affecting hundreds of thousands. Her tireless work, often on the front lines, is a masterclass in deep listening, giving voice to the marginalized, and translating their silent suffering into a powerful, undeniable call for justice that reshapes national conversations.

Sharpening your observational skills through active, empathetic listening to marginalized voices isn't just the right thing to do; it's strategically brilliant. It helps you clearly see the stark gap between what people say they value (like "opportunity" or "fairness") and what their actual policies do. That clarity reveals the precise points where you can push for real, lasting change.

**Rebel skill:** *Observational intelligence + systems thinking*

## SAM ALTMAN:
## RESHAPING THE FUTURE OF INTELLIGENCE

Sam Altman, the tech visionary leading OpenAI, uses his rebel lens to boldly challenge old ideas about intelligence, human work, and our future potential. He's at the forefront of one of the biggest tech shifts of our time: the rise of artificial intelligence, especially artificial general intelligence (AGI). In this role, he's directly confronting outdated beliefs about what human intelligence *is*, the very nature of work itself, and how innovation should be managed when technology is incredibly powerful.

Altman openly questions Silicon Valley's traditional "move fast and break things" motto. Instead, he pushes for a more cautious, collaborative approach to developing AGI. His strategy is driven by deep futures thinking and ethical foresight. He's constantly trying to imagine the long-term, widespread consequences of new tech, challenging the common belief that innovation is always neutral or automatically good for everyone. He's even engaged publicly with criticisms of capitalism and supported ideas like universal basic income (UBI), pointing out huge inefficiencies in how wealth and opportunity are currently spread around. For instance, he testified before Congress in May 2023, urging lawmakers to regulate AI and even suggested the possibility of using UBI to address potential job displacement, demonstrating a proactive stance unusual for a tech CEO. Under his leadership, OpenAI's unique "capped profit" structure is a direct attempt to reimagine how powerful technology can be developed and deployed ethically and responsibly, making sure societal benefit comes before pure, unchecked profit.

Cultivating radical skepticism means you need to get good at futures thinking and ethical foresight. Don't just assume progress is always positive. Learn to imagine and proactively tackle the long-term, ripple effects of your innovations, no matter how groundbreaking they seem.

**Rebel skill:** *Future thinking + values-based leadership*

### AVA DUVERNAY: REFRAMING NARRATIVE, RESHAPING HISTORY

Ava DuVernay, the visionary filmmaker and social justice advocate, uses her rebel lens to directly confront Hollywood's narrow, often harmful ways of portraying Black life and history. She also challenges the systemic exclusion of Black creators from the power of storytelling itself. Her films—like the historical drama *Selma*, the searing documentary *13th*, and the powerful miniseries *When They See Us*—don't just tell stories; they boldly reframe historical and current events with unflinching truth.

DuVernay exposes how media systematically reinforces racial stereotypes and twists public perception of justice and history. Her documentary *13th*, in particular, is a masterclass in systems thinking and media literacy. With incredible precision, she breaks down the US prison-industrial complex, encouraging viewers to connect the dots between slavery, the 13th Amendment, discriminatory policies that followed, and the modern era of mass incarceration. For instance, the film highlights that while the US constitutes roughly 5 percent of the world's population, it accounts for 25 percent of the world's incarcerated people, with Black Americans being disproportionately affected. She forces us to see how seemingly separate institutions are actually deeply interconnected and how narratives—the stories we consume and the ones we create—shape policy, reinforce beliefs, and ultimately determine what we perceive as "truth" or "history." Her work isn't just filmmaking; it's an act of re-education, a powerful re-narration of history from a consciously anti-establishment perspective.

Embrace media literacy and sharp systems thinking. Recognize how different institutions are interconnected and how the stories we consume, especially through media, shape our policies, strengthen our biases, and even dictate what we accept as "truth" or "history." Then, choose to tell better, truer stories—stories that challenge, inspire, and genuinely move the world forward.

**Rebel skill:** *Media literacy + pattern recognition*

## RETHINKING THE STORIES WE TELL OURSELVES

Exploring these stories of Cristina Jiménez Moreta, Sam Altman, and Ava DuVernay compels us to rethink the very narratives we've internalized. We learn to expose the often-hidden inefficiencies in existing systems—whether it's education, labor, or policy—and are compelled to propose alternatives. As sparked leaders, we're challenged to find new ways to operate, to see beyond our current reality. As the rapid rise of AI has shown us, this might mean imagining a world beyond our own, elevating our thinking to entirely new planes of consideration.

This radical skepticism isn't just for societal revolutionaries; it's intensely practical.

I once led the US storytelling effort for a 220-year-old Japanese food company—launching an unfamiliar pantry staple into a skeptical American market. The conventional approach said: Push health benefits. Normalize the weird. Blend in. But that felt like playing someone else's game.

We said: Hell no.
We used our rebel lens.

Our rebel lens told us to look beyond direct competitors and instead understand the broader context of the American pantry and family meal.

We reframed the product as ancient innovation. We didn't hide the weird—we celebrated it. We listened to *how* Americans cook, *when* they try new things, and *why* they trust heritage. We leaned into contradiction: old and new, traditional and fresh, east and west.

Our approach became about inviting curiosity rather than demanding acceptance. Instead of trying to force a new habit, we offered inspiration for integrating this ancient staple into familiar American meals. We created narratives that connected the product not just to its functionality but to a sense of culinary adventure and global connection, weaving it into the modern consumer's desire for diverse, authentic, and plant-forward options. This meant translating its traditional "umami" into a relatable "flavor secret" for home cooks. We leveraged the inherent drama of a 220-year legacy meeting a modern pantry. We didn't just market; we educated and inspired, pushing beyond simple product benefits to align with a broader belief in culinary exploration and mindful eating. We recognized that the true challenge wasn't just taste; it was overcoming the ordinary lie of what American kitchens thought they knew.

The result? The product landed not as a novelty—but as a trusted addition to the modern American pantry. Not because we forced change but because we invited it through curiosity, not conformity.

In the end, cultivating a rebel lens isn't just an intellectual exercise; it's a radical act of liberation. It means fundamentally rethinking the very stories we tell ourselves about what's possible, about who can lead, and about the true mechanics of change. This sharpened vision compels us to unceasingly expose the inefficiencies lurking in existing systems—whether it's corporate hierarchies, societal norms, community dynamics, or even the unseen routines of our own daily habits.

It's about seeing the threads of the ordinary lie everywhere, from the boardrooms dictating policy to the neighborhood group resistant to new ideas—and, yes, even within the limiting beliefs we hold about ourselves. With this lens, we're driven to propose not just viable but *transformative* alternatives for every arena. It's an undeniable challenge for us, as sparked leaders, to find rebellious new ways to operate, to carve out new pathways where none seemingly exist—whether we're innovating within a global corporation, fighting for justice on a national stage, galvanizing a local movement, or simply reshaping our own personal trajectory.

As the increasing pace of technological changes in recent years has shown us, this might mean imagining a world far beyond our current capabilities, elevating our thinking to dizzying new planes of consideration, and embracing the profound, thrilling uncertainty of what comes next. This isn't merely about adapting to the future; it's about courageously designing it—wherever you stand and however you choose to lead.

**THE REBEL LENS IS YOUR LIBERATION TOOL**

To be *sparked* is to refuse default settings. It is to burn down the status quo—not for chaos but for simplicity. It is to whisper, "There is no spoon," not just to yourself, but to your teams, your community, your culture.

You don't fix broken systems by patching them up. You fix them by seeing them *clearly*, questioning them relentlessly, and remaking them without bold assurance.

You are not a spectator. You are a rewriter of reality.

Now pick up your lens. And aim it everywhere.

**SPARK PLUG:**
**Greta Gerwig (Filmmaker) – The Subversive Storyteller**
Gerwig doesn't scream rebellion—she *embeds* it.

A filmmaker who epitomizes the rebel lens through her powerful storytelling, Greta Gerwig creates films, like *Lady Bird* or the cultural phenomenon *Barbie*, that don't just entertain; they spark hard conversations by subtly yet profoundly challenging societal norms and existing narratives around gender, identity, and ambition. Gerwig possesses an incredible observational intelligence, seeing the world differently and then reflecting it back to us in a way that feels both intimately familiar and radically new.

She takes widely accepted archetypes—the angsty teenager, the plastic doll—and uses them as Trojan horses to dissect the ordinary lies of expectation, patriarchy, and female aspiration. Her rebellion isn't loud or preachy; it's embedded in the narrative, the character choices, and the subversive humor. She makes you laugh, then makes you think, then makes you *question*. She doesn't just show us what is; she illuminates what could be, daring us to re-examine our own ingrained beliefs about gender roles, self-worth, and cultural expectations.

Her work is a masterclass in challenging rudimentary assumptions and inviting us to see beyond the limitations of our perceived reality, proving that the most impactful revolutions can sometimes be delivered with a smile and a glitter bomb.

**GET SPARKED:**
**The "Why, Why, Why Not?" Drill**
To truly embrace the rebel lens, you must learn to question everything, especially the unspoken rules and assumed truths that govern your world. This exercise helps you unearth the often-ludicrous foundations of the status quo, revealing hidden inefficiencies and exciting possibilities for radical change.

**The Prompt:**
Choose one deeply entrenched rule, rigid process, or widely accepted belief in your organization or industry. It should be something that causes mild frustration or feels "just the way it is."

**Your Challenge:**

1. Now, ask "**Why?**" at least five times, digging deeper with each answer. For example:
   - "Why do we do X?" *Because that's how it's always been done.*
   - "Why has it always been done that way?" *Because the founder believed it created efficiency.*
   - "Why did the founder believe that?" *Because in their time, technology Z didn't exist.*
   - "Why are we still operating as if technology Z doesn't exist?" *Because changing it would disrupt workflow A.*
   - "Why are we more afraid of disrupting workflow A than seeking exponential efficiency?" *Because we prioritize short-term stability over long-term innovation.*

2. After you've exhausted the "whys" and reached a fundamental (perhaps absurd) assumption, ask: "**Why not do it the exact opposite way?**" or "**Why not eliminate it entirely?**"

**Thought to Spark On:**
What surprising possibilities or systemic inefficiencies does this reveal? This exercise, though simple, is a powerful way to put on your rebel lens and begin to dismantle the ordinary lie in your own domain.

# CHAPTER 4

# THE IGNITION POINT: TAKING THE AUDACIOUS LEAP

"Do or do not. There is no try."

—*Star Wars: The Empire Strikes Back*

You've stared down the ordinary lie—that soul-numbing lullaby of safety and smallness. You've excavated your heretic purpose and polished your rebel lens to slice through the nonsense. Now comes the moment that separates dreamers from doers, the almosts from the actuals. This is the ignition point—the moment you stop circling the runway and punch full throttle.

This chapter? It's a dare. A call to arms. It involves turning your back to inertia and receiving a love letter to bold action. Because let's be real—we're all a little tired of the "you can do it" pep talks. You don't need more permission. You need a spark. So here it is.

Audacity is not optional.

"Be audacious" sounds like a bumper sticker—inspirational, forgettable, and easy to ignore. Somewhere in our spirits, we all crave a life less ordinary, a chance to leave our indelible mark on the world. But if you want to lead differently, live louder, and burn brighter, audacity is non-negotiable. It's not some Instagram quote. It's the choice to move when you're scared, to speak when it's safer to stay quiet, to act without the guarantee of applause or approval.

Audacity doesn't mean recklessness. It means courage in the face of consequence. It means choosing to risk something real in pursuit of something revolutionary. And it won't look the same in your twenties as it does in your fifties. Audacity evolves. So do you.

For me, it looked like this . . .

**MY LEAP OF FAITH: THE NETWORK NEWS GAUNTLET**

I was just a kid from the rougher side of Chicago, armed with a dream and a disturbingly bold haircut. (Thank goodness this was pre–social media!) While most people clawed their way up the ladder of local TV news, I said screw that path—I wanted to fly. I didn't want to follow the typical trajectory to a network news career. I didn't have time for the long, arduous, often circuitous route, stretching years. I was anxious to get going with my life. I needed to find a path that didn't require the usual cutting of teeth in tiny backwoods stations, followed by a slow climb through obscure, mid-size, and major markets, before even a glimmer of a shot at the big leagues. I aimed straight for *NBC News*. Ballsy. Arrogant. Yet, somehow, I landed a ten-month trial gig.

Let's be clear: This wasn't a Cinderella moment. It was a meat grinder.

I'll never forget that final interview before being hired, when I was invited into the storied, hushed offices of NBC World Headquarters at Rockefeller Center—hallowed ground for journalism. The air crackled with history and high stakes.

My first time in New York, a city that felt impossibly vast and glittering to this inner-city boy from a less fortunate part of Chicago. My first time wearing a blazer—a sartorial nod to the seriousness of the occasion. (I chose a red and black checked pattern. Ha! My misguided confidence was evident even in my fashion choices.)

I was invited to speak with the gods of broadcasting. I was corralled into a boardroom with a mahogany table that probably cost more than my childhood home. Facing me? Executive producers from *The Today Show, NBC Nightly News,* and *Meet the Press*—the heavyweights who ran America's news diet.

And there I was—a ponytail-wearing, hoop-earring'd, under-qualified nobody—being grilled like I was up for Senate confirmation. One by one, they grilled me, their questions sharp and incisive, probing my glaring lack of traditional experience. They challenged my thinking, my youthful perspectives. I had no years in local markets, no war stories from small-town news. Every question was a spotlight on my perceived deficiencies, a direct attack on my conventional résumé. This was my first full-blown battle with imposter syndrome, already a familiar background hum that now intensified into a constant static in my brain, trying to convince me I was a fraud, a fluke, utterly out of my depth.

The final question came like a sniper shot: "What will you do if we don't hire you?"

I didn't blink. "You'll be disappointed to see how well your competitor across the street will do when they hire me onto their team."

It was reckless. It was ridiculous. And it was pure, unfiltered audacity. I had no other interviews lined up, no "competitor across the street" knocking on my door. But I knew that somewhere in my gut, I could be great and do amazing things.

They hired me. That moment became my first true leap—the jump off the ledge that taught me I could fly.

Maybe you're reading this mid-burnout.

Or maybe you're still stuck in the prep phase, waiting for the "perfect time" to leap. Either way, let this be the moment you choose movement over maintenance. Not all sparks come from rage—some are born from stillness.

## FROM CONVICTION TO ACTION

There comes a moment—sometimes jarring, sometimes quietly persistent—when you feel the undeniable pull toward something more. Not just more success but more significance.

To take an audacious leap as a leader is to refuse the ordinary and step into a story only you can write. It's not a single moment of bravery; it's a series of intentional, courageous choices across the seasons of your life. It's one thing to have a brilliant idea or a fierce conviction bubbling inside. It's another entirely to step into the arena, to put that purpose into motion, to make the choices that define what you truly are. Yoda said it best: "Do or do not. There is no try." This isn't about aiming for perfection because that's often just another disguise for procrastination. This is about absolute commitment, about the raw decisiveness required to take those bold, often uncomfortable first steps toward becoming the sparked leader you're meant to be. This is where internal conviction transmutes into undeniable action—a force that moves mountains, ignites movements, and redefines your own trajectory.

Here's the truth no one tells you: Purpose is worthless without action. *Conviction without motion is just emotional clutter.* Audacious leadership isn't about feeling deeply. It's about doing bravely.

And that doing? It starts small. Tiny. Gritty. Half-baked and messy and real.

The journey from profound purpose to meaningful impact isn't a gentle stroll; it's a series of intentional leaps. Because audacity is *not* about perfection. It's about movement. Every transformed industry, every renewed organization that has found its purpose, every leader who now makes a bigger difference in their world—they all share a common turning point: the decision to act.

This isn't about blindly charging forward but about moving with clarity, conviction, and an almost insatiable willingness to try new things, experiment relentlessly, and embrace a lifestyle of courageous action.

But let's be honest about the dragon guarding this treasure. The biggest barriers to taking that first leap often live inside our heads, whispering insidious doubts. Fear of failure constructs elaborate mental prisons, convincing us that inaction is safer than risk, that embarrassment is worse than stagnation. Imposter syndrome screams that we're not smart enough, experienced enough, or worthy enough to even try—that any success is a fluke, and exposure is imminent.

And perfectionism, often mistaken for a virtue, is the most cunning trap of all, paralyzing us with the unattainable demand for flawless execution before we even begin.

Beyond our internal battles, external resistance also pushes back—the collective "we've always done it that way," the gatekeepers of the status quo, the cynics who thrive on mediocrity, and the quiet opposition of those who simply prefer things to stay the same. For a sparked leader, these aren't roadblocks to be avoided; they are crucial tests—opportunities to demonstrate the depth of their commitment to their heretic purpose.

The sparked leader moves—even when afraid, even when under-qualified, even when the voice in their head is screaming, *You're not ready.* That's how purpose becomes power.

So how do you do it?

**1. Launch the Minimum Viable Product Rebellion**

You don't need to set the world on fire today. You just need a match.

Your forward movement starts with the smallest action that puts your heretic purpose into the world. Just one move that punches convention in the gut.

Think about industry transformations: Netflix didn't immediately kill Blockbuster with a streaming empire; they started by mailing DVDs, testing a different distribution model that chipped away at the old guard. Airbnb didn't launch a global hospitality giant overnight; they rented out air mattresses in their spare room to test the concept of peer-to-peer accommodation. These were minimum viable products (MVPs) of their grand rebellion. What's your air mattress moment?

Let me show you one of mine.

Chicago was a kiln. It was the summer of '95, an unforgettable season seared into my memory. An MVP moment for sure.

The unforgiving heat wave during those months turned the city into an urban furnace. For five days that seemed to stretch on and on in mid-July, the sun hung heavy in a hazy, unmoving sky, baking sidewalks and warping the skyline in shimmering waves. Temperatures soared past 100 degrees, but the true torment came from the stifling humidity, which pushed the heat index to a staggering 120. Brick apartment buildings trapped the heat like ovens, and neighborhoods without air conditioning suffered the most. Sirens became the city's soundtrack as emergency services struggled to respond to thousands of calls, while overwhelmed morgues brought in refrigerated trucks to handle the mounting death toll. It was a crisis that exposed deep racial and economic divides, as the hardest hit were the elderly, the poor, and the isolated—those left invisible in a city teetering under the weight of its own inequalities. The 1995 Chicago heat wave was not just a weather event; it was a human tragedy that forced the city to reckon with its vulnerabilities.

It was also my first day at NBC as a field producer.

It began with the daily editorial meeting at 9 a.m., the space buzzing with veteran producers and correspondents pitching stories from all over the world. Their voices were clipped, their questions sharp, their minds already five steps ahead. The gravity of that global call was palpable. But the real sense of urgency came from the day's lead story: the biggest heat wave to have ever hit Chicago, my hometown, where I was based. The heat itself was a character, a stifling, dangerous force impacting millions. That was my first assignment. I was given a crucial portion of the story, one that would lead *NBC Nightly News* with Tom Brokaw that evening, airing nationwide. So, I once again leaned in. And that simple act became an MVP moment that would shape my outlook on life forever.

Leaning in is what sparked leaders do. We chase rebellious outcomes. The goal isn't immediate perfection but demonstrable movement. It's about creating a tiny, undeniable proof point that your idea has legs.

For instance, if your heretic purpose is to disrupt a stagnant industry with a new sustainable product, your MVP might not be a full manufacturing line with a multi-million-dollar marketing campaign. It could be a single, handmade prototype you show to a few target customers, a simple landing page to gauge interest with an email signup, or even just scheduling one crucial conversation with a potential early adopter. If you're pushing for a new policy in a nonprofit, your MVP might be a preliminary research brief, not a fully drafted legislative proposal. This small act, executed with conviction, creates momentum, gathers invaluable real-world evidence, and, critically, proves to yourself that you can take action. It shows the universe you're serious, building a psychological anchor that pulls you forward. Every tiny win combats the imposter syndrome, showing you, "Hey, I actually can do this."

**2. Cultivate a Bias for Experimentation**

Sparked leaders fail like scientists—they're curious, observant, and always learning. They don't flinch when something flops. They iterate. They adapt. They evolve.

Here's the trick: You have to treat every leap like a lab experiment.

This mindset liberates you from the paralysis of perfectionism and the suffocating fear of getting it wrong. Instead of viewing new ideas as definitive pronouncements that must be flawless from day one, you treat them as hypotheses—as experiments designed to yield learning. A renewed organization, driven by purpose, doesn't overhaul its entire system in one go. Instead, they might pilot a new process in one department, testing it with a small team; try out a new messaging approach with a limited segment of customers; or explore an alternative supply chain on a controlled scale.

Coming back to that first day at NBC.

I was introduced to my crew—a badass camera guy who looked like he had filmed the storming of the beach at Normandy and a sound tech in cowboy boots who smelled like Marlboros and magic. My marching orders from the bureau chief?

"Bring us back gold. You've got until 3 p.m."

No pressure.

Talk about imposter syndrome. It wasn't just a low hum anymore; it was a blaring siren, echoing loudly in my head: *You don't belong here. You can't do this. You're going to fail spectacularly*. My palms were sweating. My heart pounded.

Every fiber of my being screamed for a safe retreat, a chance to rewind time, to be anywhere but at the epicenter of a national news story on my very first day. I had no formal training in news production, no experience directing a crew, no real understanding of how to craft a network-level package from scratch in a matter of hours, all while under immense pressure.

But I kept going. I trusted the process. I leaned into the suck.

My sparked nature quickly rose to the surface. There was no "try" here; it was "do." Even if I failed, the urgency of the situation, the implicit trust placed in me, forced an immediate shift from paralysis to intuitive action. With nothing more than raw hutzpah and an unshakeable passion for telling compelling stories, I kept moving forward. What I lacked in experience, I made up for in sheer nerve. I called city officials. I scheduled interviews. I read the room. I listened. I faked competence.

I took on an air of confidence and know-how I absolutely did not possess. I took my basic research skills, my knowledge of how local government works, and my gut . . . and started making calls and booking interviews. Throughout that day, I took so many notes in my reporter's notebook: Lots of crossed-out ideas that wouldn't work. Lots of observations on how my crew engaged, their quiet, implied guidance influencing my choices to make sure I succeeded (thank goodness!). I figured it out on the fly, making rapid decisions about shots, interviews, and pacing, trusting my gut instincts even when logic screamed for a manual.

I told the story with sweat on my brow and fear in my gut. And I delivered.

That segment *led the broadcast.*

What a feeling. It was a baptism by fire, a visceral confirmation that taking the leap, even when terrified, was the only way forward. That the voice screaming "fraud" could be drowned out by the undeniable, tangible act of doing.

That day was my MVP. Not small in scale—but *massive* in risk, learning, and identity. A prototype for what I was capable of under pressure.

Every sparked leap is a prototype. Stop waiting for certainty. Ship it. Test. Learn. Iterate. In the end, the sparked leader embraces the intellectual sparring of these kinds of choices, each punch helping them learn how to better land the next one.

**3. Lean into the Discomfort**

Growth doesn't feel good. It feels like failure, fear, and nausea wrapped in a hoodie.

Your brain is wired for safety. Predictability. Warm blankets and Netflix reruns. But audacity? Audacity demands that you leave the cave. That you get hunted by doubt and dragged by imposter syndrome, and you still choose to show up. Taking an audacious leap means consciously pushing against that primal urge for safety. That internal churn, that knot in your stomach, that insistent voice of doubt. That discomfort is actually a powerful signal. It tells you that you're on the right track, that you're challenging the boundaries of your own perceived limitations and the ingrained norms around you. Don't let it stop you; let it be your compass, guiding you toward true growth.

The success of that first day at NBC brought a wave of relief over me. It was a heady cocktail of exhaustion and exhilaration. But here's the kicker: The imposter syndrome never truly went away throughout the five intense years that followed. It transformed, perhaps, from a blaring siren into a persistent companion, a lurking, nagging whisper always ready to point out the next potential misstep, the next way I might fall short.

Every day at NBC, I walked into a new storm. I found myself covering hurricanes, standing in the eye of the storm literally and figuratively, coordinating logistics for satellite feeds in crumbling infrastructure as chaos raged around me. I navigated the emotional minefield of school shootings, tasked with producing stories that conveyed profound human suffering with sensitivity and journalistic integrity. I was embedded in the unending grind of presidential campaigns, capturing the raw drama and unscripted moments of candidates on the stump, often working eighteen-hour days for weeks on end. I even produced segments during the pope's historic visits to the Caribbean and Mexico, navigating massive crowds, intricate security protocols, and the pressure of live global feeds.

Nothing easy. Nothing safe. And each assignment brought a fresh serving of fear. But I kept showing up.

Every assignment was a new challenge, a fresh opportunity for self-doubt to creep in, for discomfort. I kept leaning in. Although I was at the forefront of the stories that shaped our world and having a leading role to play, it was my sparked personality—that rebellious insistence on forging my own path, powered by a relentless commitment to impact—that drove me forward time and again.

I learned to quiet the noise with breath, grit, and muscle memory. I developed rebel tools:

- **Deep listening** to hear the human heart beneath the headlines.
- **Observational intelligence** to read chaos and find focus.
- **Cognitive flexibility** to pivot when plans fell apart (which they always did).
- **Values-based decision-making** to lead with integrity, even in the fog of war.

Those tools weren't downloaded. They were earned, forged in the crucible of doing.

The thrill of genuine change, the bone-deep satisfaction of impactful action, lies precisely on the other side of that initial anxiety. Embrace the jitters as a sign that you're doing something meaningful, something that truly matters. Develop mental resilience techniques: practice deep breathing to calm your nervous system, visualize successful outcomes, or break down the overwhelming feeling into smaller, manageable pieces. Celebrate the small victories, even just taking that first tiny step, to build your confidence muscle. Over time, you'll learn to recognize discomfort not as a threat but as the exciting prelude to a breakthrough, a vital part of the transformative process. This is where your personal growth truly accelerates, as you repeatedly prove to yourself that you are capable of navigating the unknown.

So when fear shows up? Don't run. Invite it in. Let it ride shotgun. Then drive away.

## THE SEASONS OF LEAPING

Audacity in leadership doesn't have to be loud. It's grounded. It's the quiet decision to act when others hesitate. It's refusing to shrink from possibility. It's choosing growth over fear, creativity over convention, and service over safety.

So, what if the life you're living isn't the one you're meant for but the one you've merely settled into? Maybe what you need is a spark to get things going, to push you off that complacent track you're on: *Chase success, avoid failure, stay in bounds*.

Your audacity will evolve. So will the shape of your leap. We often experience our leadership journey in distinct "seasons," each presenting unique opportunities and challenges for that crucial ignition point.

The leap isn't a one-time event. It's a rhythm, a cycle, a sacred choreography that evolves with you. Sparked leaders don't just leap once. They leap in every season.

### IGNITION (20s to 30s | The Season of Becoming)

This is the season of raw energy, clumsy action, and unapologetic experimentation. You don't know who you are—and that's your advantage.

You're testing ideas, challenging norms, and actively deciding who you are—and who you are emphatically *not*. You're feeling your first sparks, those undeniable urges to break free. The audacious leaps here often involve daring to choose a calling over convention, launching something before you feel "ready," or walking away from paths that no longer fit. It's about advocating fiercely for your values in spaces that resist them and saying a resounding "yes" to what feels risky but real.

So, learn to say yes before you're ready. Quit what doesn't fit. Make noise. Burn drafts. Choose fire.

If this is your season, keep asking yourself: *What if I don't need to follow* their *script?*

**ASCENT (40s to 50s | The Season of Refinement)**
You've earned some clout. Now ask yourself if you're using it well. This is where comfort becomes a trap.

Here, the leap is not about proving your worth but about strategically aligning your accumulated influence with your deepest values. You might be leaving a position of stability to pursue a more profound purpose, reclaiming creative dreams once set aside, or restructuring your entire life to genuinely reflect what matters most. This is the season for speaking uncomfortable truths from a position of leadership or perhaps investing deeply in others' growth as a conscious act of legacy-building.

You don't need more titles. You need alignment. Strip the excess. Speak bolder. Mentor louder. Pivot harder.

It's time for a serious analysis: *Am I climbing the right mountain?*

**RESONANCE (60+ | The Season of Amplification)**
You're not fading—you're thundering. This is your time to pour it out.

Sparked leaders don't wind down; they turn outward. This is the season of pouring out wisdom, living boldly in newfound freedom, and making impact that echoes through generations. It's legacy not as a finish line but as a living, breathing offering to the world. This phase allows you to reimagine your influence in new, unexpected ways. You're able to tell your unfiltered story, not for accolades but to empower others. Giving away your time, knowledge, or platform with radical generosity fuels you, and you want to advocate fiercely for justice, peace, and future generations. During your resonance, you are embodying courage and clarity in every conversation, every choice.

Tell the unvarnished truth. Build for others. Challenge power. Legacy isn't a plaque; it's your life as a megaphone.

The driving question here: *How can my life still change the world?*

These seasons don't follow a neat timeline. You might leap backward to leap forward. We all move at our own pace, and elements can overlap or appear out of sequence. But they are potent invitations. At any moment, you can choose to ignite, ascend, or resonate in new ways. You can be a sparked leader. It's a pattern of showing up differently—more fully—and saying to yourself: *I will not waste this life. Disrupting comfort can create change.* And *I will be brave enough to lead where others won't go.*

But make no mistake—every season calls for motion.

**FINAL CALL: CHOOSE BOLD**

This is your ignition point. The crossroad where good intentions die or get activated.

The sparked life? It's not handed to you. You claim it—with callused hands, trembling voice, and relentless fire. You leap. You learn. You leap again.

You choose to disrupt the dull.

To rewrite the rules.
To light a match in a room soaked in kerosene.

So, the only question left is: Are you ready to jump?

**SPARK PLUG:**
**Reshma Saujani (Girls Who Code) – Leaping Against the Grain**
Reshma Saujani didn't wait for tech to fix itself. She torched the playbook.

The journey of the visionary founder of Girls Who Code embodies the audacious leap against immense skepticism and a deeply entrenched gender gap in technology. Saujani didn't wait for permission; she saw a glaring problem—the alarmingly low number of women in computing—and chose to act with steadfast conviction.

After an unsuccessful political campaign, many might have retreated, licking their wounds and rethinking their approach to public life. But Saujani, driven by a heretic purpose to close the gender gap in tech, pivoted decisively. She didn't just see a lack of women; she observed a systemic issue: Girls were simply not being exposed to computer science in engaging ways during their formative years, and the industry's culture itself wasn't welcoming or inclusive once they did enter. Her leap was unexpected; she decided to build a groundbreaking organization from scratch, creating a pipeline and a supportive community for future female technologists.

She faced skepticism, not just from established tech giants who were content with the status quo but also from venture capitalists who doubted the "market" for teaching girls to code, seeing it as a niche, nonprofit endeavor rather than a scalable solution. Educational institutions were often locked into traditional curricula, resistant to change. There was a prevailing mindset that coding was "for boys" and that girls simply weren't interested.

Despite these formidable headwinds, her unfaltering perseverance, combined with a clear, compelling vision, allowed her to launch initial summer immersion programs and club networks. She built momentum step by step, proving the demand and the profound impact these programs could have on young lives. Girls Who Code grew into a national and even international movement, reaching millions of girls and intrinsically reshaping perceptions about who belongs in tech, inspiring countless others to follow suit.

Saujani didn't just advocate for change; she *created* the change, proving that a single courageous step, driven by a radical purpose, can ignite a massive, industry-wide transformation.

That's what sparked leadership looks like. That's the audacious leap.

**GET SPARKED:**

**The Smallest Giant Leap**

It's easy to admire audacious leaps from a distance, but the true sparked leader takes them. This exercise is designed to help you break down that daunting "big idea" into an immediate, actionable step, transforming internal conviction into undeniable forward momentum.

**The Prompt:**

Based on your heretic purpose (from Chapter 2) or a convention you've questioned (from Chapter 3), identify one idea that feels exciting but also slightly too big or risky to pursue. This is your audacious leap.

**Your Challenge:**

Now, break it down: What is the single, absolute smallest but bold first step you could take on this idea within the next forty-eight hours? It doesn't have to guarantee success, just initiate movement. It might be:

- Sending one email to a person you admire or someone who could offer a key insight.
- Blocking out thirty minutes in your calendar to deep-dive research a specific, critical aspect of the idea.
- Writing down the first three bullet points of a preliminary action plan.
- Asking one provocative question in your next team meeting that directly challenges the status quo related to your idea.
- Telling one trusted friend or colleague about your "crazy" idea and asking for their honest, unfiltered feedback.
- Drafting a single sentence that concisely articulates the core problem your idea aims to solve.
- Scheduling a fifteen-minute coffee chat with someone outside your immediate circle who might have a different perspective on your idea.

**Thought to Spark On:**

Commit to taking that step. Do it. Then, reflect on how it feels to initiate. Notice the shift from thinking to doing. That feeling? That's the ignition point. It's the moment you stop "trying" and start *doing*.

# PART II

# FAN THE FLAMES

*How rebellion scales—through teams, culture, and creative fire.*

# CHAPTER 5

# FANNING THE FLAMES: IGNITING DECISIVE ACTION IN YOUR TEAMS

"Where we're going, we don't need roads."

—*Back to the Future*

You've dismantled the ordinary lie, unearthed your heretic purpose, and sharpened your rebel lens. You've even made the terrifying, exhilarating audacious leap.

Now what?

Here's the rebel reality: Being a sparked leader isn't a solo sport. It's not enough to burn bright. You must become the matchstick that lights the whole forest. The goal isn't to rebel alone—it's to lead a rebellion that others can't ignore.

Think you can change the world by yourself? Cute.

The real flex is sparking others so powerfully that they carry the flame farther than you ever could. That's leadership. That's legacy. That's where sparks turn systemic.

I'm inspired by the choices made by Sal Khan, the visionary who dared to rewrite the rules of education with Khan Academy.

He didn't start with a Silicon Valley war room or a bold brand manifesto. He started by tutoring his cousin. That's it. No money. No master plan. Just a spark.

But that spark? It refused to stay small.

He saw what personalized learning could do. He saw the brokenness of an education system built on rigidity and access gaps. And instead of hoarding the solution, he handed it out freely, purposefully. That spark leapt from one kid to millions, from one laptop to classrooms and communities across the planet. He didn't lead with ego. He led with purpose. He didn't build a brand. He built a movement.

That's your playbook.

This chapter is your ignition point for others. The strike pad that turns your personal flame into collective combustion. Because rebellion, when done right, is wildly contagious.

We're not talking passive delegation. This is leadership that unleashes.

It's about crafting a vision so potent, so unshakably clear, that others don't just follow it—they *fight* for it. It's about creating a culture where autonomy isn't a perk—it's the power source. Where your team doesn't wait to be told—they can't wait to act. Where your spark becomes *theirs*.

Sparked leaders don't build armies. They build co-conspirators.

They don't just assign tasks. They cultivate ownership. They create climates where innovation isn't a buzzword—it's muscle memory. Where bold ideas don't need permission—they just need ignition.

Because where we're headed? There are no maps. Only paths we scorch into existence together.

Let's light it up.

## LEADING BEYOND SELF: EARLY ENCOUNTERS WITH COLLECTIVE IGNITION

I've never been a mayor. Never sat in the senate. But I've always dreamed of leading in a way that moves people, shifts systems, and lights the sky. Not the tangled, cynical politics of modern service but the pure, aspirational ideal of public service, of being a unifying force for profound, positive change. I knew early on that leadership roles, no matter the scale, were where true impact could be made, where the levers of change were truly accessible.

My first taste of that? Sixth grade. Classroom president. The keys to my kingdom: the hall pass. My weapon: a glimmer of purpose. Even then, a tiny flame of responsibility, a nascent desire to serve, however small the domain, flickered within me.

Later, in college, I chaired the junior/senior banquet committee. This wasn't about picking a DJ (though getting that right was an existential crisis for social standing and crucial for attendance!). What set me ablaze was delivering a message that mattered. That did it. Sparked! I got high off the idea of moving a crowd. Not for applause but for impact. The feeling of crafting a message that truly resonated, that inspired a collective sense of purpose, was a potent, addictive charge. It felt like I was weaving magic with words, pulling disparate threads of individual ambition into a shared tapestry.

Fast forward: My alma mater calls. They want me on the alumni board.

I didn't show up to sip bad coffee.

Soon enough, propelled by that same inner drive, I found myself on the leadership team and, in short order, became its president. I showed up to shake the system; it was about injecting a vibrant, new pulse into a role that had historically been largely symbolic. I formed subcommittees, pressed issues, demanded action. I went where voices were needed, not wanted. I didn't know I was being sparked then, not by name, but I did know that I felt an undeniable, almost physical, compulsion to act, to push, to constantly improve. And yeah, I got under some skin. But I also got results. A century-old institution started listening differently. Eventually, they even asked me to lead crisis communications. (Spoiler: That gig ended fast. Turns out relentless drive isn't always welcome. Lesson learned, spark retained.) But the impression was made. The culture shifted. And I walked away knowing I lit a fire.

One of the most valuable takeaways from this intensely active season of life was the sheer, magnetic power of motivating others toward action, of sparking a collective will. A lot of the influence I generated wasn't just about the ideas that sprang directly from my own mind. It was equally about challenging others in my immediate circle—my fellow board members, alumni, even students—to also raise their own voices, to volunteer their precious time, or to want to be deeply involved. It was about translating my personal spark into a shared, undeniable flame that drew others into the fray.

Leadership for me has always been about ignition. Not spotlight. Not ego. Just spark. And that spark? It spreads best when shared.

At a global marketing firm, I tore apart stale team structures. Not to control them but to set people free. Dream bigger. Act bolder. Own it. As a leaned-in, motivated dreamer myself, I wanted to spark action and ignite creativity throughout the entire team, making their potential explode.

But a tension as old as mankind quickly reared its head: collaboration versus control. This, I learned, is another treacherous area where sparked leaders need to find immense clarity and consistently refine their approach.

You want impact? You've gotta get real about how you lead. Because sparks don't survive in suffocating environments.

## THE SANDBOX DILEMMA: LEADING WITH VISION, NOT DOMINATION

You can build the biggest, boldest brand in the world—but forget who owns the sandbox, and it all crumbles.

Sparked leaders don't bulldoze. They co-create.

We don't lead in a vacuum. Whether it's a team, an organization, a community group, or a family, your biggest impact happens when your spark becomes a shared flame. And that only happens through trust, purpose, and collaboration.

Here's the critical truth: It's not enough to have a big idea. You have to work in a way that brings others with you. How you lead is just as important as what you're building. It's the essential bridge between individual genius and collective transformation.

Take Google's Project Aristotle—a deep dive into what makes teams thrive. This multi-year study into what truly makes teams effective found that it wasn't intelligence or charisma that stood out. It was psychological safety. People felt free to speak up, fail, experiment. Teams ignited not from top-down control but from an environment of trust and openness. It's a stark reminder that even the most revolutionary vision requires collective buy-in and genuine collaboration to truly ignite.

Creating that kind of space? That's on you.

If you're already a sparked leader at the helm of a team or group, this is your invitation to level up. This isn't just about ensuring your brilliant ideas see the light of day; it's about mastering the art of leading and guiding with impact. We're talking about the critical importance of clarity amidst authority, of unleashing passionate motivation even when faced with a multitude of approaches.

Here's how:

- **Anchor your vision so others can run with it.** The clearer and more compelling your "why," the more confidently others can experiment within it. Think of your vision as the foundation—when people know what matters most, they'll innovate without losing direction.
- **Clarify the outcome. Let them choose the method.** The best leaders don't dictate every step. They build the frame and let others paint the picture. You're not here to micromanage—you're here to unleash.
- **Don't confuse clarity with control.** In my world as a marketer, I've built brilliant campaigns that flopped because I forgot who shared ownership. If I steamroll over the existing culture or fail to bring others into the process, the whole thing crumbles. Collaboration

> is oxygen. I learned this the hard way. At one agency, I pushed too hard, too fast. I didn't read the room. I brought vision but no listening. The result? Friction, resistance, breakdown. That wasn't rebellion—it was ego. I wasn't igniting others; I was shutting them down.

Sparked leaders thrive in community. Being a motivated, leaned-in individual can already scare people enough. Tamping down the ego, making genuine space for others, can be the critical difference between transformational impact and being just another has-been attempt to change the status quo. Listening, adapting, making room for co-creation enables us to avoid our internal Warhol tendencies—that desire to be the sole artistic genius—and instead craft outcomes and solutions that resonate more deeply because they are truly co-owned.

This is not an invitation to be bland, boring, or expected. This is simply a reminder that there is more than one way to achieve revolutionary results. Being a collaborative spark increases the likelihood that your transformative ideas take hold and flourish because they have a multitude of champions, not just you.

Sparked leaders make space. They bring people in. They don't sacrifice vision—they share power. That's how movements are born. That's how sparks become wildfires.

Before we charge forward, take a breath.

Think about the spaces where you've truly been seen. Where your voice wasn't just heard—it mattered.

How often have you had to code-switch, dim, or dodge? How often did you decide it was safer to shrink than to shine?

Now imagine a world where your leadership doesn't require translation.

That's where we're headed.

## THE ART OF COLLECTIVE IGNITION: PRINCIPLES FOR FANNING THE FLAMES

As sparked leaders, our commitment to driving systemic change—no matter how big the system—demands more than just our personal brilliance. It requires us to become master architects of collective effort capable of igniting decisive action in our teams and communities.

Sparked leadership isn't about micromanagement. It's about leading by sparking curiosity, fostering difference, and supporting others to reach their own ignition points.

It's about movement-building. Let's break it down:

### 1. Articulate a Revolutionary Vision, Not Just a Plan

A sparked leader doesn't just communicate goals; they paint a vivid picture of a transformed future. Your team needs to see, feel, and believe in the world your heretic purpose is trying to create. This means:

- **Beyond the "What," Focus on the "Why":** Purpose beats projects. Always.

  Continuously tie every project, every pivot, every seemingly mundane task back to the core purpose. Why does this matter? What problem are we truly solving? What essential belief drives this effort?

- **Storytelling as Your Core Tool:** Data persuades. Stories ignite.

A sparked leader understands that facts convince but stories move. You don't just present data; you craft a compelling narrative—complete with a burning problem, an aspiring hero (your team or customer), a formidable villain (the status quo or a daunting challenge), and a vision of a triumphant future. This infuses your vision with imagery and emotional resonance, making it unforgettable and sticky.

Think back to any major Apple product launch, especially during Steve Jobs's era. They didn't just rattle off technical specifications. When the original iPod was introduced, Jobs didn't lead with gigabytes and processing speed. Instead, he painted a vivid picture of liberation: a thousand songs in your pocket. He connected a sleek device to a universal desire for music on demand without the clunky limitations of CDs or bulky players.

The problem was clear: Music was tethered. The hero was *you*, the music lover. The villain was the inconvenient, fragmented music experience. And the triumphant future? Your entire music library effortlessly with you, everywhere. With the iPhone, it wasn't just a phone, an iPod, and an internet communicator; it was "one device" that revolutionized how you lived, worked, and connected. Apple didn't sell phones; they sold freedom, creativity, and connection. They understood that the most potent way to ignite decisive action isn't through bullet points but through a story that makes people *feel* the future you're inviting them to create.

- **Make It Shared:** Don't impose vision. Invite co-ownership.

A revolutionary vision isn't a decree handed down from on high; it's an urgent, compelling invitation. To truly ignite decisive action, you have to involve your team in refining that vision, letting their insights, their unique perspectives, and their personal aspirations deepen its richness. This means creating dedicated workshops where everyone can contribute, actively soliciting diverse feedback through open forums, or even establishing small, cross-functional vision teams. When individuals actively contribute to the vision's creation, they don't just understand it intellectually; they own its pursuit, becoming fiercely committed co-creators rather than mere implementers. This shared ownership transforms compliance into genuine conviction.

**2. Foster Autonomy and Cultivate Psychological Safety**

For teams to truly lean in and transform, they need both the freedom to act and the safety to fail. This is where you create the conditions for decisive action.

- **Set Boundaries, Then Step Back:** Let them own the how.

  Define the clear "sandbox" (the vision, the core values, the ultimate outcome) but empower your team to play freely within it. Provide direction, then step back and trust their expertise.

- **Celebrate Experimentation:** Fail forward. Loudly.

  A sparked leader understands that innovation is rarely a straight line; it's a messy, iterative process fueled by bold attempts and invaluable lessons. So, actively encourage your team to try new things, even if they might not work on the first (or fifth) try. Celebrate the learning from "failures" as much as the successes. Make it genuinely safe to say, "This didn't work as planned, but here's exactly what we learned."

Have you heard of Google's legendary "20 percent time" policy? Some saw it as a quirky perk, but it was truly a radical act of trust and a direct invitation for employees to experiment. Google essentially told its engineers: "Spend one day a week on *anything* you're passionate about, even if it has nothing to do with your core job description." This wasn't about control; it was about unleashing latent potential. From this seemingly chaotic freedom, game-changing innovations like Gmail, AdSense, and Google Maps didn't just emerge—they *exploded*. Google wasn't asking for compliance; they were cultivating an internal culture of forward-leaning experimentation, betting that curiosity, given permission and safety, would yield far more breakthroughs than rigid oversight ever could. It's a powerful testament to how a leader's willingness to embrace calculated risks in others can ignite unexpected revolutions.

- **Create Feedback Loops:** Make candor a muscle, not a minefield.

Create a culture where honest feedback is given and received with the intention of growth, not blame. This goes beyond annual reviews; it's about building continuous, low-stakes channels for communication. Think of it as a constant calibration of your team's compass, not just a yearly audit. Psychological safety is the bedrock here, is crucial for radical transformation. It's allowing individuals to speak up, share concerns, and challenge ideas without fear of reprisal, which is crucial for radical transformation. This also means actively soliciting diverse perspectives, creating safe spaces for dissent, and demonstrating that you, as the leader, are open to receiving critical feedback and adapting your own approach.

**3. Build Trust Through Transparency and Co-Creation**

Vision without trust is just a dream. To ignite decisive action, your team needs to trust *you* and trust *each other*.

- **Be Radically Honest:** Even when it hurts.

  This isn't about spilling every secret but rather about fostering profound trust. Share the "why" behind decisions, even the tough ones that might cause discomfort. Explain the challenges you're facing, the uncertainties you're navigating, and the difficult trade-offs that have to be made. For instance, if a strategic pivot means scaling back a popular initiative, don't just announce the change; openly share the market shifts or resource constraints that necessitated the decision, along with the projected long-term benefits. This level of honesty—even when it's hard—builds immense respect and cultivates genuine co-ownership, transforming passive recipients of news into active partners in the journey.

- **Share Strategy, Not Just Tasks:** Co-create the path.

  Involve team members in strategic decision-making, not just execution. When they contribute to the strategy, they are invested in the outcome. When a victory occurs, ensure credit is shared widely and authentically.

- **Elevate Diverse Voices:** Innovation lives in the messy middle.

Don't just delegate tasks; invite team members to actively shape solutions with you. This isn't about politeness; it's about elevating their sense of purpose and harnessing a multitude of diverse perspectives, leading to richer, more resilient, and truly groundbreaking outcomes.

At IDEO, the legendary design firm, they don't just solve problems; they invent solutions through a process that looks, at times, gloriously chaotic. When faced with a complex design challenge, they don't lock a lone genius in a room. Instead, they bring together designers, engineers, anthropologists, marketers—sometimes even the client's customers—for rapid prototyping and highly collaborative brainstorming sessions. The walls get covered in Post-it notes, ideas are sketched roughly, prototypes are built and torn down within hours. It's noisy and messy and requires a profound trust that the best ideas don't emerge from a singular vision but from the friction and fusion of collective intelligence. IDEO's sparked leaders understand that true innovation isn't built in isolation; it's co-created in the vibrant, sometimes uncomfortable space where diverse minds are given permission to play, experiment, and build together.

**4. Overcome Internal Resistance with Empathy and Clarity**

Even within a committed team, resistance to change can emerge. It's often rooted in fear, not malice.

- **Listen Deeply:** Surface objections hide deeper fears.

  This is more than just waiting for your turn to speak. It's about deploying your deep listening skills to uncover the *real* reasons for resistance, which are almost never the ones stated upfront. People might voice concerns about "process," but beneath that, you might find a profound fear of the unknown, a genuine concern about job security in a changing landscape, a deep-seated pride in old ways that have served them well for decades, or simply a fundamental misunderstanding of the vision you're championing. For example, when introducing a new technology, a team member might say, "It's too complicated," when their deeper fear is, "Will this make my job obsolete?" As a sparked leader, your job is to listen beyond the words, to hear the underlying emotions and unspoken anxieties, because only then can you truly address the root cause of resistance and begin to build bridges of understanding.

- **Address the Real Pain:** Name it. Own it. Walk through it.

  Don't dismiss concerns; acknowledge them. True transformation often creates anxiety, and a sparked leader understands that fear, if unaddressed, will suffocate even the most brilliant initiative. Your role is to provide tangible support, robust training, and relentlessly clear communication to help bridge the daunting gap from the old, familiar ways to the new, uncertain future.

  Imagine you're working on a community initiative to replace an old, beloved, but ultimately unsafe public park playground with a new, modern, and inclusive design. An "ordinary" community leader might just announce the change, perhaps with a bland rendering and a brief public meeting. But a sparked leader recognizes the underlying fear—fear of losing cherished memories, concern about the unknown safety of new materials, or even a sense of being unheard. They don't just mandate the new design; they craft a narrative around its necessity and its benefits for *all* families, emphasizing safety, accessibility, and new play opportunities for every child. They then invest heavily in community engagement, not as a formality but as an empowering journey, providing open design workshops where neighbors can contribute ideas, accessible prototype sessions for kids to test new equipment, and regular town halls where concerns are genuinely heard and addressed. They anticipate common pain points (like temporary park closure or changes to familiar structures) and proactively provide accessible support channels—a dedicated community liaison, clear construction timelines, and celebratory events highlighting the future benefits. By directly confronting the fears with empathy and practical solutions, the sparked leader transforms potential resistance into engagement, converting skepticism into shared excitement and pride in their new community space.

- **Show the Win:** Paint the better future—tangibly.

  Clearly articulate how the revolutionary vision will ultimately benefit individuals and the team, not just the organization. Show them the tangible improvement, the increased fulfillment, or the greater impact that lies beyond the discomfort of change.

**5. Celebrate Micro-Rebellions and Learning Agility**

Sustaining momentum and fostering a culture of continuous audacity requires celebrating the small steps and the learning moments, not just the massive breakthroughs.

- **Praise Bravery, Not Just Results:** Trying IS winning.

  Recognize and praise individuals and teams not just for success, but for the bravery to experiment, to take risks, and to challenge the status quo, regardless of the outcome.

- **Extract Insights Publicly:** Normalize the pivot.

  When an experiment doesn't yield the desired result, it's tempting for teams to gloss over it or even hide it away. But a sparked leader actively embraces these moments, transforming perceived failures into invaluable learning opportunities. Instead of focusing solely on the outcome, shift the conversation to what was learned from the experience. What new insight was gained that you wouldn't have discovered otherwise? What previously held assumption was definitively debunked? This isn't about sugarcoating; it's about rigorous analysis. By publicly dissecting the process—not the person—and drawing out concrete lessons, you reinforce the value of bold experimentation itself. This creates a safe environment where teams feel empowered to take calculated risks, knowing that every attempt, successful or not, contributes to the collective wisdom and moves the needle forward.

- **Tell the Stories:** Culture is shaped by the tales we tell.

  Regularly tell stories, big and small, about how team members used their rebel lens or took an audacious leap. These narratives don't just inform; they become powerful cultural touchstones, inspiring others and reinforcing the desired behaviors.

At Zappos, the online shoe and clothing retailer, they are renowned for their radical customer service and unique company culture. Early in its journey, Zappos made a seemingly counterintuitive move that cemented its commitment to its core values: After new hires completed their initial training, the company famously offered them $2,000 to quit. This wasn't a cost-cutting measure; it was a deliberate act by their sparked leadership to filter out anyone who wasn't truly committed to their "WOW" customer service and unconventional culture. It was a test of conviction, not just skill. This seemingly radical policy became a legendary story within and beyond the company, a powerful narrative about Zappos's staunch dedication to cultural fit above all else. It wasn't just a policy; it was a story of defiance against the conventional wisdom of holding on to every hire, transforming a bold decision into an enduring lesson that inspired deep loyalty and reinforced their unique vision.

So, ready to build impossible things with improbable teams?

Remember: Real revolutions don't come from lone wolves. They come from leaders who spark a thousand others and then get out of the way. It begins with the clarity to pinpoint your goal, the cojones to motivate profound engagement, the relentless drive to obsess over every vital detail, the humility to make expansive room for groundbreaking ideas, and then . . . the courage to let it go.

Because in the end, your legacy isn't what you build. It's what you *ignite*.

**SPARK PLUG:**
**Ryan Coogler (Filmmaker) – Creative Conviction at Scale**
Throughout this book, our spark plugs illuminate the path forward. These are not just success stories; they are portraits of individuals who initially grappled with the very ordinary lie we've discussed—the seductive pull of complacency, the soul-crushing routine, the pressure to conform. But something within them rebelled. They found their dissident path, proving that the spark isn't inherited; it's ignited through conscious choice and bold action.

Ryan Coogler isn't just a generational talent—he's a transformational leader. His story isn't about talent alone. It's about refusal . . . to sand down his edges, to make his stories more "palatable." It's about refusal to accept the ordinary lie that says success requires assimilation. At every turn, Coogler has rejected complacency in favor of conviction. From *Fruitvale Station* on, he's chosen specificity over safety, truth over trend, and community-rooted storytelling over industry expectations. That refusal hasn't just delivered great films—it's rewriting what Hollywood considers viable, bankable, and worthy of attention.

But Coogler's real brilliance isn't just *what* he makes—it's *how* he makes it. His films—from *Creed* to *Black Panther* to *Sinners*—aren't solo acts. They're collective rebellions. Coogler invites costume designers, musicians, historians, dialect coaches, and young actors into a shared mission. He doesn't hoard vision—he distributes it. He doesn't dominate the sandbox—he expands it. He creates the psychological safety for bold ideas to thrive, honors lived experience as creative capital, and trusts his people to bring their whole selves into the work.

That's why the impact of his work doesn't stop at the screen. *Sinners* didn't end when the credits rolled. That's when it sparked. It became a cultural accelerant. With the most Oscar nominations ever for a single film, it cracked open conversations about representation, mental health, faith, race, gender, justice, and joy. It rippled into fashion, music, policy, and purpose, and it did so because Coogler leads from conviction. He reminds us that when one person refuses to conform, others feel permission to do the same. And when refusal becomes collective, culture doesn't just shift—it rises up and roars . . . Let that sink in.

**GET SPARKED:**
**The Compelling Call to Arms**

As a sparked leader, articulating your vision isn't just about informing; it's about igniting. This exercise challenges you to condense your revolutionary idea into a compelling call to action, designed to bypass complacency and drive commitment in others.

**The Prompt:**

Imagine you have just sixty seconds—a single, urgent minute—to inspire your team (or a group of peers or even your family) to embrace your heretic purpose or a revolutionary idea you've identified. How would you articulate the burning problem you're solving and the extraordinary future you envision in a way that bypasses mere compliance and ignites genuine, unshakeable commitment?

**Your Challenge:**

Write out your sixty-second "call to arms," focusing on passion and impact over facts and figures. Think:

1. **The Provocation:** What's the ordinary lie you're challenging?
2. **The Heretic Purpose:** What's the bold, new reality you envision?
3. **The Call to Action:** What single, compelling action do you want them to take or embrace *with* you?
4. **The Emotional Hook:** What feeling do you want to leave them with?

**Thought to Spark On:**

This isn't about memorizing a script; it's about finding the core, undeniable truth of your vision and delivering it with the raw conviction that compels others to join your rebellion.

# CHAPTER 6

# THE KALEIDOSCOPE OF IMPACT: LEADING THROUGH DIVERSE IGNITION

"A great artist can come from anywhere."

—*Ratatouille*

We're still not done ratcheting things up toward next-level rebellion. Are you ready to become the most dangerous, unstoppable leader who doesn't just spark fire in curated rooms? Ready to build infernos in the wild—where real life is raw, messy, and unfiltered? Ready to cultivate wildfire from the glorious, multicultural kaleidoscope of humanity.

This chapter? It's not about playing it safe or clean. It's about diving headfirst into the vibrant chaos of humanity and choosing to lead *from within it*—not above it. It's about leading with your sleeves rolled up, your senses on high alert, and your heart cracked wide open.

Because here's the truth they don't print in leadership books: Sterile strategy doesn't spark revolutions. Culture does. Conflict does. Community does. When you draw power from the full spectrum of human experiences—race, gender, class, ability, belief, identity—you stop designing solutions that *serve* people and start co-creating ones that *belong* to them.

The best ideas? They're not hiding in PowerPoints. They're pulsing through block parties, shouted across church basements, whispered in hair salons, coded into murals, cooked into street food, and humming in the playlists of kids rewriting the future in real time. And they're waiting for you to show up with open eyes and fearless ears.

So, bring your full self. Not the polished one—the real one. Listen louder. Lead deeper. Build wider. Because sparked leadership doesn't tidy up the world—it unleashes it.

**THE URBAN SPARK: CULTURE AS FUEL, NOT FRICTION**

As a first-gen Puerto Rican kid in Humboldt Park, Chicago, my world was a dizzying remix of tradition, transition, and tectonic cultural shifts.

At home, the rhythm of salsa music filled the air, the kitchen was alive with the scent of tropical foods like *arroz con gandules* and *pernil*, and family talk was always in Spanish. Our conversations were incessantly punctuated by the dramatic crescendos of telenovelas mixed in with the wholesome narratives of *TGIF* comedies on ABC. The TV became a literal portal, pulling me between two realities.

Outside, the streets were a living canvas: hip-hop break battles on the street corners, defiant beats of salsa and merengue spilling out of windows, white kids blasting Blink-182, and the newest reggaeton bangers pulsing from every passing car.

I didn't just passively absorb these sounds or experiences; I lived within them as a constant cultural sponge. I plucked ideas and insights wherever I could: new foods to enjoy, different expressions to weave into my vocabulary, exposure to fashion trends and styles so different from what was worn at home. I wasn't just bilingual—I was bicultural, bi-coded, and born into a lifelong rhythm of code-switching. I grew up reading people and cultures like open books. What started as survival became strategy. As a professional, it became my differentiator.

This mash-up upbringing didn't just make me adaptable; it made me observant. The nuances I absorbed at dinner tables and street corners now fuels marketing strategies, social campaigns, and organizational culture shifts. It made me see the human thread before the business pitch. It's why I could design "Sobre Mesa" influencer dinners—born from Puerto Rican table conversations over *arroz, platanos,* and *pasteles,* and evolved into brand activations across US cities. They weren't gimmicks; they were extensions of lived truth.

Seeking the counsel of elders, something deeply engrained from my summers with Abuelita in Puerto Rico throughout my high school years, is another one of the foundational insights that have challenged my work as a strategist on numerous occasions. As modern and progressive as I like to make my thinking, I often find myself also making sure my clients don't forget their history. I always honor where they came from.

My life has been a crash course in seeing the threads that connect us all, a skill that has become my secret weapon as a leader.

Your spark might've come from a different zip code or cultural mash-up, but the principle remains: The wider your lens, the sharper your aim.

**LEADING WITH YOUR STOMACH (AND SOUL)**

Throughout my career, I've learned the most profound leadership lessons with a fork in hand. In Bali, Berlin, or Buenos Aires or back home in Río Piedras, the way people eat reveals how they live, how they love, and what they value. For me, a deliberate practice of eating like the locals do—seeking out the holes-in-the-wall, the bustling local haunts, and the vibrant street markets—has fueled me.

I'm not talking Yelp reviews—I'm talking emotional intelligence. Social strategy. Leadership IQ.

This isn't a food tour for my palate; it's a masterclass in leadership, where every dish and every shared table becomes a classroom. This simple habit has challenged my assumptions and enabled me to engage with the chaotic kaleidoscope of culture that fuels true innovation. It's been a purposeful act of stepping into someone else's world to find the common threads that connect us all.

My elbow-to-elbow wurst meals in Berlin taught me about collective pace and shared discomfort. A champagne intermission queue during a theatre performance in London taught me the elegance of order in chaos. Communal meals in Bali, where I devoured the best fried rice anywhere (*Nasi Goring!*), were powerful reminders that we can easily get along and find connections, whether in shared, close quarters while dining or at events that bring the masses together when promoting a new product.

Street food in Thailand reminded me to seek flavor in the margins. Sharing slow, relaxed tapas in Madrid, where the conversation lingers as long as the wine, delivered an appreciation for the art of chill—and the necessity of lingering a bit longer in thought. I've applied that to creative development, letting ideas marinate before rushing them out into the world.

And the simple, friendly banter at a food counter—my most repeated lesson reinforced time and again over a proper mofongo back home in Puerto Rico—has kept the idea of being real, being present, being *accessible* front of mind. That principle echoes in every campaign I design, every story I write, every room I lead.

Each plate came with unspoken wisdom. And that wisdom became creative insight, brand direction, team management style. Leadership that's disconnected from human ritual is sterile. Sparked leadership lives in the flavor, the banter, the tension. It's in the moments you almost miss.

And by the way—those food journeys and passport stamps? They're not some humble brag. Take them as a challenge. You can build your own table. You can carve out your own path. I didn't manifest these opportunities—I poured deep, blistering, sweet equity into every single one. The mileage status? That's just the bonus.

## THREE PRINCIPLES OF KALEIDOSCOPIC LEADERSHIP

Let's break it down. This chapter isn't a postcard—it's the heart of our playbook.

The world isn't a flat, monochromatic landscape. It's a dynamic, often chaotic kaleidoscope of ideas, emotions, and experiences—and your greatest leadership potential lies in learning how to deliberately look at it, not just through your own lens but through a multitude of others. This is about taking the blinders off. It's a deliberate, no-holds-barred commitment to leveraging every day and every experience—from a family dinner to a new country's public transit—to fuel your inner being and sharpen your mental capacities.

When you do this, you show up more intentionally and have more profound impact because you're operating from a place of deep understanding as opposed to a default assumption. In fact, cutting-edge research consistently backs this up.

Many studies have shown that highly empathetic companies can outperform their less empathetic counterparts in productivity, earnings, and growth by over 50 percent. This kind of deep, compassion-driven understanding isn't just a "soft skill"; it's a strategic superpower that drives innovation and unlocks the full potential of diverse teams.

Your goal as a sparked leader is to stop passively absorbing your surroundings and start actively plucking insights from the world around you.

Here are three unflinching principles for leading with lived diversity and global truth:

**1. Radical Presence: Train Yourself to See**

Every room you walk into is a goldmine of unspoken signals. Most people are too distracted to notice. Not you. Radical presence means ditching autopilot and choosing to observe like your life depends on it.

My habit of traveling and eating what the locals eat was never just about the food. It's about the ritual, the environment, and the people around me. This is the heart of radical presence. It's the conscious choice to be fully immersed in the moment, observing and listening with a beginner's mind. It's how you train yourself to see the profound in the mundane and the universal in the unique. You learn to read the world like a book written in a thousand different languages—some spoken, most not.

What you see when you pay attention beyond the surface is pure, unvarnished insight. It's a lens you should apply as you navigate the world around you. Next time you're in a group setting, don't just wait for your turn to talk. Instead, actively observe the unspoken tensions, the nonverbal cues, and the group dynamics. Who defers to whom? Who speaks, and who is silenced? These radical observations give you the precise information you need to engage with purpose—to create space for a quiet voice, to address a hidden conflict, to make a silly joke, or to challenge groupthink in new ways. Activate this approach in your work environment, perhaps by adding walk and talk meetings with team members that allow them to share their insights in less stressful environments or more casual encounters.

Your trip to the grocery store or a visit to the local park are not just routines; they are rich data streams. By consciously observing these moments, you can discover unspoken needs or powerful, uncelebrated rituals. You're learning to identify not just moments but signals. They tell you where your leadership is needed, where a gap exists, or where a hidden resource is waiting to be activated.

When you practice radical presence, you can observe your own default assumptions, your moments of frustration, or the creative blocks you've been avoiding. You might realize your stress isn't from the task itself but rather from a mental model you're using to approach it.

The more you practice being present in these small moments, the more you'll train your mind to pull out profound insights that others simply miss. This is how you stop just reacting to the world and start intentionally influencing it.

**Challenge:** Pick one mundane moment this week—a commute, lunch, a Zoom call—and treat it like an anthropological dig. What did you notice that others missed?

**2. Cultural Code-Switching: Rewire the Room**

I grew up with required fluency in multiple worlds all at once—home was all-Spanish conversations and salsa music on the speakers; school was a swirl of social norms in a diverse urban classroom; the streets taught me how to read tone, vibe, and gut instinct more than grammar. And this was all before I ever stepped into a workplace, where yet another set of codes defined how to show up and be heard. This constant shifting between perspectives taught me that understanding is a fluid art.

Code-switching isn't a burden—it's a superpower. It's how you connect across divides, translate between worlds, and remix ideas that weren't meant to mingle. It's what allows you to find deeper, more profound commonalities rather than simply surface-level distinctions. In my career, it's made me more adaptable and more resonant, able to build ideas that cut through the noise because they're rooted in a shared humanity.

Think Shonda Rhimes, a creative titan who built an entertainment empire. Her success isn't just due to her genius for high-drama storytelling; it's rooted in her unapologetic commitment to centering diverse voices and perspectives.

Her writers' rooms aren't diverse because it's trendy; they're diverse because it's essential. Real stories need real voices. She fuses high drama with real-life nuance and explodes old TV tropes. That's rebellion. She's proved that by embracing the different shades of human experience, you can create stories that not only captivate but also unite, building bridges where others only see walls of separation.

I applied this thinking at the plant-based food company. Recognizing that we were a Japanese brand being sold in the States, I guided our package development to include cultural cues from our heritage in the design, honoring ideas that were born in Japan but that were applicable for Americans. It worked. Consumers liked the fusion. Shoppers embraced the "foreign" as flavorful and appreciated the unknown as an opportunity to expand awareness. And just like that, a cultural gap became a bridge.

**Challenge:** Cross a border—professionally or personally. Talk to someone outside your echo chamber. Learn how they see the world. When you engage, try to understand their worldview—their values, their priorities, their language—not to judge but to learn. Look for the underlying human commonalities, not the surface-level distinctions. Use that insight to reshape a project, a pitch, a policy.

### 3. Intentional Exposure: Curate Your Inputs

How hard do you work to be someone who passively absorbs your surroundings? Do you actively seek out new experiences (*carpe diem*—remember that?), personal experiments in cultural exploration? For me, it's been a mixed life of comic books and Shakespeare, traditional food and global street fare, all forging my diverse outlook. It's built a foundation of intentional exposure. It's a deliberate act of seeking out inputs that challenge your existing reality and broaden your mental models, ensuring your thinking never grows stale.

That being said, don't wait for brilliance to show up in your feed. Go seek it. Read outside your comfort zone. Follow artists you don't understand. Sit in on a worship service that isn't your own. Let discomfort positively rewire your brain.

Innovation doesn't come from comfort. It comes from curiosity. The more friction you allow into your worldview, the more sparks you'll create.

**Challenge:** Add one new input to your week—a book, a podcast, a restaurant, a conversation—that challenges your norm. Follow thinkers on social media who challenge your political or social beliefs. Try a new food, listen to a new genre of music, or visit a neighborhood you've never been to before. These small acts of intentional exposure become invaluable fuel for your mind, filling your creative well with fresh perspectives. They empower you to develop ideas that don't just speak to your echo chamber—they resonate with the beautiful, complex world beyond it.

By applying these principles, you begin to see every conversation, every interaction, and every new experience as not just another moment in your day but a chance to glean a unique spark. You stop waiting for big, revelatory journeys to land in your lap and start treating your entire life as the raw material for leadership and impact.

## TRANSLATING EXPOSURE INTO FIREPOWER

Cultivating a radical presence, mastering cultural code-switching, and living with intentional exposure aren't just intellectual exercises. They are the essential work of a sparked leader preparing for a creative rebellion.

Once you've filled your mind with these nuggets of observation—the shared experience of a crowded food stall, the rhythm of a different city's public transit, the unspoken rules of a new culture—it's time to learn how to actively use them. Your rebel lens isn't just for seeing; it's for building. This is where you transform passive inspiration into transformative action, crafting unique solutions that resonate because they're founded in a deeper, richer understanding of the world.

Here's how to grab those insights from the kaleidoscope of your life and forge them into something that creates a profound impact:

**Misfit Ideas – Borrowing Brilliance:** This is the art of recognizing a successful solution in one context and courageously applying it to a completely different one. It's about seeing the fundamental principle behind an idea, not just its form, and asking: *Where else could this work?*

The magic is in the analogical thinking.

A powerful example of this played out in Porto Alegre, Brazil, in the late 1980s. A group of radical democratic leaders introduced the idea of participatory budgeting, a simple but revolutionary concept: empower ordinary citizens to directly decide how a portion of the public budget would be spent. An "ordinary" politician might have dismissed this as too radical or too chaotic for their own country's context. But a sparked leader recognizes the core principle—civic empowerment through shared decision-making—and courageously adapts it. The result? This "misfit" idea has been successfully borrowed and adopted in thousands of cities around the world, from New York to Paris, leading to increased civic engagement, more equitable resource allocation, and a profound rebuilding of trust between local government and its people.

The magic of analogical thinking isn't limited to civics. Just consider how Ukrainian President Volodymyr Zelenskyy, a former comedian and actor, leveraged his professional background to reinvent political campaigning. When he was looking for new representatives for his political party, he and his team opened up candidate selection to everyday citizens via an online "audition" process. Applicants submitted video pitches explaining why they should represent their districts; the best of these were then posted publicly and voted on through a smartphone app—directly borrowing the talent show mechanics that made his hit TV series so engaging. This approach shattered the gatekeeping norms of party politics, turning Ukrainians into active participants instead of observers. It resulted in them winning 254 of 450 parliamentary seats, an unprecedented majority for a first-time political movement. Zelenskyy showed exactly how a "misfit" idea from one arena can be repurposed to spark real-world change.

You can apply this same analogical thinking to your work and life:

- **For the Business Leader:** Say you work for a company facing a slow, frustrating internal process. Perhaps you recall the elegant efficiency of a European queue at a local market, where everyone patiently waits their turn.

Your insight isn't to make your team stand in a line. Instead, you adapt the principle: You create a simple, respectful digital queue for submissions, providing clarity and reducing chaos, thereby transforming a source of workplace tension into a model of fair collaboration.

- **For the Community Leader:** Suppose you're looking for ways to foster neighborly connection in a sprawling, anonymous suburb. You might recall the tight-knit, elbow-to-elbow camaraderie of a bustling food stall in another country. Your ultimate solution, then, isn't to force everyone to eat together. You borrow the concept of physical proximity and shared experience. You advocate for communal seating in the local park, a shared garden plot, or a community tool library, creating natural spaces for connection to happen.

**Unspoken Needs – Finding the Problem No One Mentions:** Look beneath surface complaints. What are people really hungry for? Dignity? Belonging? Time? Your rebel lens must read between the lines. A deep, radical presence allows you to pick up on the subtle frustrations and unmet needs that are rarely articulated out loud. People often get so used to an inconvenience that they stop noticing it. As a sparked leader, you use your observational skills to find these quiet cracks in the system and fill them with a groundbreaking solution.

Imagine a university campus where students constantly complain about bureaucratic processes—long lines for registration, confusing financial aid forms, and a general feeling of being a faceless number. Their stated frustration is the inefficiency. But the unspoken need, which a sparked leader with a rebel lens would uncover, is a deeper cry for respect, for a system that sees them as individuals, not transactions. It's a craving for efficiency, yes, but more so, it's a desire for a sense of belonging and care from the institution. By listening to the tone behind the complaints—the weary sighs, the eye rolls, the expressions of powerlessness—a student leader could move beyond simply creating a new online form. They could propose a peer-to-peer mentorship program or an ombudsman role, directly addressing the underlying feeling of being lost in the system. The solution isn't just about process; it's about people.

The same principle applies across every arena of life.

- **For the Business Leader:** Say your team complains about endless meetings, but they don't see a way out. Through deep listening, you recognize the unspoken need isn't for *fewer* meetings but for more *purposeful* ones. Your solution is to create a new "agile meeting" format: stand-up huddles, visual whiteboarding, and a policy that if an agenda isn't clear, the meeting is canceled. You've solved the unspoken problem of inefficiency, not just the stated problem of too many meetings.
- **For the Individual:** Imagine you notice your friends are all stressed and overwhelmed by social media, but they feel obligated to keep up. Maybe, then, your insight is to organize a monthly Saturday Morning Digital-Free Hang—a group that meets once a month with phones turned off, sharing stories face-to-face over a meal (or a café con leche if you're inviting me). You've addressed a deep, unspoken need for genuine connection and mental space.

**Hybrid Solutions – Fusing Worlds for Unprecedented Innovation:** Fuse the old and the new, the traditional and the disruptive. This is the ultimate expression of cultural code-switching. You draw from your diverse experiences and combine them to create a solution that is both familiar and revolutionary.

One of the most striking examples of this concept is Peloton, which took the centuries-old stationary bicycle and fused it with live-streaming video, onboard computing, and a subscription model to create an entirely new "immersive connected fitness" service. Peloton's first bike (launched in 2014) packed a high-definition touchscreen and Wi-Fi into the frame, allowing users to join live classes or choose from on-demand workouts filmed in Peloton's studios. Rather than just selling hardware, Peloton sells a continuous content subscription—melding equipment, software, and community into one ongoing experience. Peloton team spent roughly eighteen months prototyping this system—combining hardware design, a bespoke operating system, and a network-delivered class platform—so that riders could get the boutique studio experience at home. That fusion turned a one-time exercise bike purchase into a sticky, recurring revenue service and effectively created a brand-new market category.

All that being said, let's be clear: This isn't about veering into cultural appropriation or disrespect. A sparked leader doesn't simply grab a trend from one culture and slap it onto another. Instead, they lead with genuine curiosity and a profound respect for the source. This type of rebellious creativity is rooted in deep listening, a collaborative spirit, and a humble acknowledgment that you are not the sole authority. The goal is to build a bridge, not to borrow a costume. It's about fusing principles with permission, celebrating shared insights, and co-creating with the very communities that inspire you.

- **For the Business Leader:** Maybe your challenge is to make a legacy brand feel relevant to a younger, multicultural audience. Don't abandon the brand's history. Instead, fuse its core values (e.g., tradition, quality) with the vibrant, fluid aesthetics of a new culture you've experienced, creating a marketing campaign that honors the past while speaking directly to the future. You might combine classic brand messaging with the fast-paced, irreverent humor of a new social media platform, creating a "hybrid solution" that feels both authentic and fresh.
- **For the Community Leader:** If you're trying to spark civic engagement in a community with a large, diverse population, you can fuse the formal, structural models of traditional town halls with the vibrant, communal storytelling circles you've observed in another culture. You create "Community Story Circles"—a hybrid forum where formal proposals are shared, but community members are first invited to relay personal stories and experiences related to the issue. You've blended structure with emotion, policy with humanity, creating a space where everyone feels seen and heard.

By actively engaging in this creative rebellion, you begin to see that your unique blend of life experiences isn't just who you are; it's your raw material, your secret weapon. This is the kaleidoscope of leadership: fractured, colorful, messy—and unbelievably powerful.

Your job isn't to flatten it. It's to flip it, rotate it, and find the pattern only you were meant to see. Then spark others to see it too.

**SPARK PLUG:**

**Bad Bunny (Musician/Cultural Icon) – The Global Rebel of Authenticity**

Let's talk about more about Bad Bunny—not just as a genre-bending musician but as a global *cultural insurgent*. This isn't your garden-variety celebrity. Bad Bunny is a full-blown *revolution* dressed in mesh tops, painted nails, and an unshakable swagger that dares the world to challenge his right to exist loudly, colorfully, and without permission.

Benito Antonio Martínez Ocasio launched from grocery store bagger in Puerto Rico to *planetary force* without asking for anyone's blessing. And that's the point. He didn't climb some sanitized industry ladder. He *torched it*—opting instead to rap in Spanish, reject Eurocentric beauty norms, embrace gender-fluid fashion, and build a brand rooted in an unfiltered identity fueled by his culture, his politics, and his people.

But it's not just his music—it's how he shows up.

Nowhere was his rebel flame more potent than during his 2025 Residency Takeover in Puerto Rico—a summer-long cultural detonation that turned an entire homeland into a stage, a movement, a megaphone. This wasn't a concert series. It was an act of valiant reclamation. Sold-out shows and a who's-who of collabs who all came to rub shoulders during this legendary run injected pride, purpose, and power back into a colonized island that is too often exploited and overlooked. Bad Bunny didn't just perform *for* Puerto Rico. He performed *with* Puerto Rico.

That residency made global headlines—but more importantly, it made local impact. Economic boost? Absolutely. Cultural affirmation? You better believe it. But deeper still, it was rebellious healing. A reminder that Puerto Rico isn't just worthy of attention—it's a *beacon*. Bad Bunny's presence said: *We define ourselves. We center our stories. We take up space in the center of the map.*

He's proof that a leader doesn't need a title to spark a movement. You just need the courage to live fully lit—rooted in identity, fluent in rebellion, and unafraid to disrupt comfort zones, even (and especially) your own.

Bad Bunny never tried to fit in. He didn't have to. He just built his own universe—and dared the world to catch up.

**GET SPARKED:**

**The Unexpected Spark-Seeker**

To truly embrace the wide range of impact, you must actively seek out and value perspectives that are radically different from your own. This exercise challenges you to break out of your intellectual echo chamber and deliberately seek insights from unexpected places.

**The Prompt:**

Identify a current challenge or new initiative you're working on. It could be a professional project, a personal goal, or a community issue.

**Your Challenge:**

Intentionally seek input on this challenge from at least three individuals who have radically different backgrounds, expertise, or roles than your own. Think outside your usual circle. This might mean:

- Someone from a different department or industry.

- A younger or older colleague or friend.
- A parent or community elder.
- Someone with a completely different hobby or life experience (e.g., a musician, a farmer, a graphic novelist).

What unexpected insight or "spark" did their unique perspective bring to your challenge that you wouldn't have found otherwise? How did their different background or worldview force you to re-examine an assumption, consider a new angle, or see a possibility you had previously overlooked?

**Thought to Spark On:**
The greatest innovations often happen at the intersection of unexpected ideas. Your job as a sparked leader isn't just to have the answers—it's to know where to find the questions you didn't even know you should be asking.

# PART III

# BUILD THE BLAZE

*Where rebellion becomes movement—and systems start to sweat.*

# CHAPTER 7

# BEYOND THE BOUNDS: SPARKING SYSTEMIC CHANGE

"Sometimes you gotta break the rules
to make things right."

—*Silver Linings Playbook*

That line isn't just clever. It's gospel for sparked leaders. Because here's the unvarnished truth: The "rules" we live under—policies, traditions, hierarchies, and institutional blueprints—are all human-made. They weren't handed down on stone tablets. They were invented. Which means they can be challenged, dismantled, and reimagined.

For a sparked leader, that realization isn't a footnote. It's the inflection point. Up to now, we've tended the internal fire: stoked rebellion, forged heretic purpose, and made the audacious leap. But this chapter is where we ask the real question: Will you contain that spark, or will you let that fire be directed outward? Will you let it blaze beyond your personal circle to challenge the larger systems that shape how we live, work, and thrive?

This is your passport to go *beyond the bounds*—beyond the polished veneer of incrementalism, beyond the outdated playbooks of tradition, beyond the resignation of "this is just how things are." You're here to question the scaffolding that props up the status quo and redraw it with purpose-soaked fire.

This isn't about swapping one broken process for another or issuing another set of repackaged ideas. This is about torching assumptions that no longer serve, surfacing the ordinary lies we've accepted as truth, and rewriting the rules themselves. Surviving the system isn't victory. Reinventing it is.

I bet you're ready to strike the damn match already! We're almost there. A bit more kindling and some gasoline before we get the fire going.

**A CASE STUDY IN REINVENTION: THE LIBERAL ARTS UPRISING**

It's one thing to quote movie lines about breaking rules. It's another thing entirely to stand at the edge of a one-hundred-year-old institution, watching it teeter on the brink, and realize the rulebook that built it is now dragging it down.

That was the moment facing a small, century-old liberal arts college in a rural town. Crushed by declining enrollment, rising costs, and a shifting student landscape, the school faced the same death spiral devouring peers across the country. Some had lasted generations, surviving wars and recessions. But now the rules they trusted had become shackles, calcified into anchors.

When I arrived, the air was heavy with resignation. Every strategy session recycled tired ideas: rebrand this, tweak that. "Innovation" was a facelift on a fossil. Every "new" solution was really an old one dressed up in fresh language. It was déjà vu masquerading as strategy. The staff clung to rituals that felt holy but were, in truth, toxic.

What they couldn't see? The very traditions they thought would save them were suffocating their future.

Tinkering wasn't an option. It was lethal.

So, we broke the oldest rule in the building: "Stay in your lane."

We shattered silos. Departments that hadn't shared oxygen in decades sat at the same table. Faculty and marketers stopped glaring and started co-creating. Ideas were borrowed from tech, hospitality, retail—places academia used to scoff at. What emerged wasn't just a fresh campaign. It was a bold new model.

And yeah, it was uncomfortable for a while. Rule-breaking always is. But slowly, sparks caught. Vision expanded. Trust was rebuilt. Relationships shifted. Marketing stopped being "the megaphone" and started being a thought partner. Faculty stopped being "keepers of the ivory tower" and started being architects of a shared mission.

The rules had been broken. And thank God they were.

The turnaround isn't complete, but the trajectory is clear: enrollment trending upward, cooperation across silos. And something radical took root: shared purpose. Most importantly, the institution no longer sees itself as a victim of decline but as an author of its own reinvention.

It was living proof of that line from *Silver Linings Playbook*. Sometimes, you really do have to break the rules to make things right.

## STILLNESS BEFORE THE STORM

Systems don't topple in a day. They don't flinch at a single scream. But every spark counts—every whisper, every refusal, every fracture in the wall.

What comes next?
It's not just about burning brighter.
It's about burning wider. Louder. Smarter.

Take a breath.

Because we're not just lighting fires anymore—we're aiming them.

## THE SPARKED PLAYBOOK FOR SYSTEMIC CHANGE

Systemic change isn't just about policy. It's about possibility. It's not a to-do list—it's a full-body jailbreak.

Your goal isn't to fix around the edges. It's to challenge the assumptions baked into the system itself. Sometimes that means tweaking policies. More often, it means tearing up the page and starting with a new headline: *Make it better.*

Think of it like moving from a rigid, classical score to an improvised symphony. Instead of following the same sheet music everyone else has been playing for decades, sparked leaders learn to hear the whole orchestra differently—shifting perspectives, bringing in new instruments, and inviting others to join the performance.

Let's dive into the details of how sparked leaders do it:

### 1. Shift the Lens: Break the Linear Score

Forget linear. Forget logic. Sparked leaders start at the end: *What would wild success look like if nothing stood in the way?*

True systemic change begins with perspective. This isn't just about solving a problem for users; it's about fundamentally reshaping the conditions in which the whole system operates. Most organizations follow a rigid, linear score: problem (verse), solution (chorus), implementation (ending). Sparked leaders refuse to play this predictable tune. They begin in the middle, envisioning the ideal outcome, and then rewrite the opening measures to match it.

Maybe if we spend time sitting in the middle first—envisioning the ideal outcome without regard for the current roadblocks—a new, more fearless beginning will become clearer. This isn't fantasy; it's design thinking, a liberation from the inertia of the present.

Take Airbnb. The initial problem they were looking to address wasn't "how do we get more hotel rooms?" It was "how might we create a world where anyone can belong anywhere?" By focusing on that ideal outcome first, they didn't just compete with hotels; they reimagined the very nature of travel and hospitality itself.

**2. Reframe Empathy: Hear the Whole Stage**

Empathy isn't just about listening to customers. It's about hearing the *entire orchestra*.

A sparked leader widens the stage—they don't only focus on the soloist. You listen for the percussion of employees, the strings of regulators, the brass of funders, the woodwinds of community voices.

True empathy is orchestral. You're not just identifying pain points. You're mapping power, tension, and opportunity.

You're understanding the roles people play, the incentives that drive them, and the constraints they face. It's about blending empathy with systems awareness, prototypes with pilot programs, and iteration with cultural learning. Tools like stakeholder interviews, journey mapping across silos, and systems mapping help uncover these dynamics and create a holistic view of the system you're trying to shift.

Indra Nooyi, the former CEO of PepsiCo, took on a massive, established system from the inside out. For decades, PepsiCo's business model was simple: sell as much sugar-laden soda and junk food as possible. It was a wildly profitable but inherently unsustainable system.

Nooyi saw this and, driven by a heretic purpose, chose to rewire the whole business. She empathized with the broader system—the health crisis, the environmental impact, and the changing values of a new generation of consumers. Her "Performance with Purpose" strategy was a system-aware approach that re-envisioned PepsiCo's role in the world, shifting its portfolio toward healthier products and sustainable practices.

This wasn't an easy move, but it was prophetic. It was a deeply unpopular, often ridiculed bet that long-term purpose would outperform short-term profits. She persisted, and today, "Performance with Purpose" is a guiding principle for the entire industry, proving that even the most entrenched systems can be reshaped from within by a leader with an bold, unwavering vision.

If empathy is the ignition point for systemic change, Ai-jen Poo turned it into an engine. As founder of the

National Domestic Workers Alliance, she saw the invisible labor holding America together—the caregivers, housekeepers, and nannies long dismissed as "help."

Her rebellion began in living rooms, not boardrooms, listening to stories others ignored. Through patient organizing, she reframed "care" from being a private duty to being a public good, mobilizing a multiracial coalition that won landmark protections, including the National Domestic Workers Bill of Rights.

Poo's genius wasn't protest for protest's sake—it was design. Her leadership shows what happens when you go beyond the bounds of traditional activism. She translated compassion into policy, narrative, and infrastructure, giving domestic workers both dignity and political power. Her heretic purpose was simple but radical: to make care visible, valuable, and protected. In doing so, she didn't just change laws; she rewired how a nation understands work, worth, and the invisible systems that keep it running. Empathy, in her hands, became revolution . . . and the world is still catching up.

**3. Borrow New Instruments**

Sometimes your orchestra needs more than new notes—it needs new instruments. Sparked leaders borrow, steal, and adapt tools from everywhere. They're pirates of progress.

Going beyond the bounds might mean:

- **Analyzing different industries for analogous challenges:** How did a hospital streamline patient intake? How did a restaurant chain scale its operations? These "misfit analogies" can unlock a solution for a seemingly unrelated problem.

- **Experiencing different geographies:** Travel isn't just for pleasure; it's a form of active research. How do other cultures handle communication, partnerships, or resource allocation?
- **Engaging with new voices:** As we saw in Chapter 6, unexpected insights reside with individuals who are completely outside your usual circle.

Ultimately, this moves you from a purely human-centered approach to a system-aware one. While you must always keep people at the core, you recognize that change isn't a memo; it's muscle memory rewritten.

The key questions become not only "what's desirable?" but also "what's feasible within this system?" and "what's sustainable long term?" Going beyond the bounds means refusing to stay in your echo chamber.

This isn't just cross-pollination. It's systemic synesthesia—seeing hidden patterns, adapting foreign solutions, fusing disciplines.

The real question isn't, "Is it innovative?" It's: "Does it serve, scale, and last?"

**4. Facilitate Collective Ownership: Invite the Orchestra In**

As a sparked leader, you're not a soloist. You're a conductor *and* a student. Sparked leaders design the process itself as transformation.

Furthermore, sparked leaders don't conduct alone. They turn the process itself into a rehearsal where everyone plays. It requires collective buy-in and co-authorship. Design labs, workshops, and co-creation spaces don't just generate solutions—they break down silos, build trust, and craft new shared narratives. This allows for a deeper and more meaningful commitment from everyone involved.

Yes, it's scary, challenging, and confusing to hand the baton to others. But systems don't change because of one conductor's will. They change when the orchestra itself learns to play a new song together. Beyond the bounds, the leader isn't the hero of the story. The system itself becomes the stage, and everyone plays a role in rewriting the script.

When everyone owns the change, it *sticks*. When everyone scores the new music, the orchestra plays like it's theirs.

But rebellion isn't only built in theory—it shows up in people. Let me show you.

**The Peril of the Status Quo: A Tale of Two Companies**

Systemic change isn't just a bold choice; it's often a necessity for survival. Businesses that fail to innovate, that choose to remain in the comfort of the status quo, are often replaced by those who dare to go beyond the bounds. History reminds us that systems don't collapse overnight—they erode under the weight of complacency. The average lifespan of a company on the S&P 500 index has plummeted from over sixty years in the 1950s to under twenty years today. The reason? A failure to adapt, to change without purpose, or a stubborn insistence on "business as usual."

In the mid-nineties, Boston Chicken was a thriving business built on a single, high-quality offering: rotisserie chicken. They had a clear value proposition, a loyal customer base, and a repeatable process that made them a local favorite. But they grew complacent and, in a fit of overreach, made a fatal miscalculation. They rebranded to Boston Market, attempting to become a full-service, American-style restaurant with a vast, unfocused menu.

This wasn't a reinvention driven by purpose; it was a panicked attempt to chase a larger market. In their ambition, they diluted their core identity and, most critically, alienated the very customers who loved them for their simplicity and quality rotisserie chicken. Their downfall was a direct result of trying to be everything to everyone instead of being something truly special to their people. They failed to go beyond the bounds with a heretic purpose. Instead of reimagining their successful model for a new era, they threw away what made them unique, leading to a spectacular bankruptcy and a hard-fought return to their original, focused purpose. Their story stands as a stark warning: Change without a clear purpose isn't progress—it's a betrayal of what makes you special. Boston Chicken's collapse shows what happens when a system loses its heretic pulse. Purpose is replaced by panic.

Leaders who choose to innovate with purpose, not just for the sake of it, stand in stark contrast to those who cling to the status quo. These are the individuals who understand that true transformation requires a core conviction that outweighs tradition.

Here are two leaders who didn't just break the rules—they drafted blueprints for insurgency:

**Jacinda Ardern: Leadership Through Crisis**

Jacinda Ardern, the former prime minister of New Zealand, demonstrated the power of a sparked leader in a systemic crisis. When faced with a series of national tragedies, including the Christchurch mosque shootings and the White Island volcano eruption, she didn't rely on a traditional political playbook of stoicism and hard power. Instead, she chose to lead with radical empathy, vulnerability, and a profound focus on unity. She wore a hijab in solidarity with the Muslim community, directly confronted hate speech with a human-first approach, and embraced a message of compassion. Her leadership, rooted in a deep sense of connection, became a new model for how a nation could heal in the face of profound grief. She went beyond the bounds of political tradition, proving that emotional intelligence and humanity are powerful tools for systemic change.

**Wendy Kopp: Innovate with Purpose**

Wendy Kopp, the founder of Teach For America, also demonstrates the power of making impactful change by coloring outside the lines. Like Indra Nooyi at PepsiCo, Kopp confronted a massive, entrenched system: public education. The traditional playbook for addressing educational inequity focused on slow, long-term policy reform. At the same time, top college graduates rarely considered teaching a desirable career, making it difficult for under-resourced schools to find high-quality educators.

Kopp's heretic purpose was to reframe the problem and rewrite the rules. She believed that top college graduates, if recruited and trained effectively, could make a profound impact in high-need classrooms, even with a short-term commitment. Her idea was irreverent: create a temporary teacher corps, a "Performance with Purpose" model for education. She didn't wait for the system to fix itself; she built a parallel, purpose-driven pipeline.

This idea was deeply unpopular and widely criticized in its early days. Many in the education establishment saw it as a temporary fix that devalued the teaching profession. But Kopp's unwavering commitment to her purpose—providing all children with an excellent education—persisted. Her innovation wasn't just the program itself but the framing of teaching as a form of social activism and a competitive, respected career path for bright young leaders. She created a new model that brought thousands of talented individuals into the education system, and many went on to become lifelong advocates and leaders in the field. She proved that a single, bold idea, driven by a fierce purpose, can reshape an entire industry and spark a massive, systemic shift.

Ardern proved that empathy could rewrite the rules of governance, while Kopp showed that audacity can rewrite the rules of education.

But don't get it twisted. These weren't random acts of inspiration. These were *engineered uprisings*. Fueled by fire, yes—but sustained by strategy.

**ORGANIZED REBELLION**

Rebellion without a plan? That's just noise.

But rebellion with intention? That's how systems shake. That's how blueprints get rewritten. That's how revolutions endure.

If you want your rebellion to last, it needs more than fire—it needs form. Vision. Stamina. Spreadsheets.

I still cringe thinking about a client I once coached—a bold, visionary leader running a scrappy enterprise with real potential. They were scaling quickly and knew they needed help at the top. So they brought on a new CFO. He was earnest. Hungry. Affordable. And completely out of his depth.

He'd never operated at the C-suite level before, but he was eager to prove himself. That eagerness came with blind spots. To "keep things simple," he started rounding up when it came to tracking monthly earnings and expenses. It didn't seem like a big deal—until it was. When year-end reconciliation hit, the numbers were off by tens of thousands of dollars. Critical infrastructure upgrades had to be delayed. Staff raises that had been promised were suddenly off the table. The damage wasn't just financial—it was relational. The trust cost more to rebuild than the budget gap itself.

It wasn't sabotage (I think). It was the absence of systems. No shared budget templates. No calendarized reviews. No accountability scaffolding to catch the errors before they compounded.

In another instance, a lack of dashboards cost a different team thousands in avoidable write-offs. They hadn't built shared systems to track production against sales and inventory—or even expiration dates. One analyst failed to update the other. Neither checked in with finance or logistics. Suddenly, the warehouse was sitting on a six-month supply for a three-month sales commitment. Perishable product—gone to waste.

No one was watching closely enough—and they didn't have the right tools in place to catch it in time.

The lesson? Fire without form is failure waiting to happen. Systems don't slow you down—they keep you from crashing.

Passion without a framework is a firecracker . . . it pops, flashes, and fizzles. A sparked rebellion? That's designed to *burn through the night*.

This doesn't mean playing it safe. It means playing it smart. Not winging it—but wielding it.

Wielding your purpose like a scalpel.
Your voice like a call to arms.
Your process like a battle plan.

I'm not asking you to adopt someone else's system. We're challenging you to build your own. Flexible enough to evolve. Strong enough to scale. Rooted in values that don't bend under pressure.

Because if you don't build a system, you'll be trapped inside someone else's.
And most of those weren't built for your brilliance.

So, what's your plan?
What are you building that outlives your charisma?
Where does your rebellion find its rhythm?

We've scattered the ingredients throughout this entire book. The fire, the frameworks, the fundamentals. But only you can assemble the engine. (I hope you're not waiting for me to shape that too . . . that's for another book. Or for when you hire me as your strategic consultant.)

This is *your* movement. Give it a backbone.

**THE FINAL STEP: REWRITING THE RULES**

Rules may tell you to stay in your lane, to play the same notes, to never stray from the score. Sparked leaders refuse. They break the rules, rewrite the music, and lead the world in a new song.

Exploring these stories helps us recognize that the "rules" of any system—be it a college, a political party, or a global corporation—are simply constructs, not eternal truths. Systems last only as long as we *believe* in them. The moment we stop, we open the gates to transformation.

For a sparked leader, the goal isn't to simply function within the system but to identify its essential flaws and, with courageous purpose, question it, rewrite it, reinvent it.

Improvement and betterment are only possible when we dare to question, when we dare to confront our own assumptions and expectations. Change isn't just possible. It's waiting for your engagement.

This means imagining a world beyond our current capabilities, elevating our thinking to new planes of consideration. It also means remembering that at the heart of our drive for change is a commitment to making the world better for people. It's about not just adapting to the future but courageously designing it.

Now go—beyond the bounds, past the limits. What are you waiting for?

**SPARK PLUG:**
**Wangari Maathai (Kenya) – The Defiant Seed-Planter**

Let's end with one more rebel, one who didn't just challenge a system but who rewrote it from the roots up.

Wangari Maathai didn't just plant trees—she planted defiance. She rewrote the rules of how environmental, economic, and political systems interact. Through the Green Belt Movement, she saw what others missed: Deforestation wasn't simply an environmental problem. It was the root system feeding multiple crises—soil erosion that destroyed crops, poverty that disempowered communities, gender inequality that silenced women, and political oppression that thrived on people's disconnection from the land.

Her solution was as radical as it was simple: empower women to plant trees. At face value, it looked like an act of environmental stewardship. In reality, it was a systemic intervention. Every seed carried multiple layers of defiance—against ecological collapse, against patriarchal structures that denied women agency, against corrupt governments that profited from exploitation. The act of planting a tree restored land, generated income, gave women a voice, and rebalanced power in local communities.

In 2004, Maathai became the first African woman to win the Nobel Peace Prize. She was duly honored for her "holistic approach to sustainable development that embraces democracy, human rights, and women's rights in particular." Her legacy shows that systemic change doesn't always require a massive policy overhaul or sweeping technology. Sometimes it begins with one courageous act that cuts across systems, disrupting the whole web of assumptions that held them in place.

Wangari Maathai reminds us that the most profound systemic shifts often start with a single, defiant seed.

**GET SPARKED:**

**The Systemic Shockwave**

To be a sparked leader is to not just identify problems but to see them as systems ripe for reinvention. This exercise challenges you to pinpoint a system's core assumption and imagine a single spark that could set off a chain reaction of change.

**The Prompt:**

Choose a specific system, process, or industry paradigm that you believe is ripe for disruption. What's the one small yet strategically positioned "spark" or intervention you could introduce that, if successful, would send a shockwave through that system and fundamentally challenge its core assumptions?

**Your Challenge:**

Think of examples like Netflix's shift from DVDs to streaming, which challenged the core assumption of physical media ownership, or Uber's peer-to-peer model, which challenged the assumption that taxi companies needed to own their vehicles. Now, for the system you've chosen:

- **Identify the Core Assumption:** What's the ordinary lie that everyone in this system accepts as truth?
- **Define Your Spark:** What is the one small, daring leap you could take that directly challenges that assumption?
- **Sketch the Shockwave:** What would be the potential ripple effect of this single, targeted spark? How would it force other parts of the system to adapt, change, or fall apart?

**Thought to Spark On:**

The biggest changes don't always begin with an earthquake. They often start with a single, perfectly placed tremor.

# CHAPTER 8

# SUSTAINING THE FIRE: THE RELENTLESS PURSUIT OF NEW HORIZONS

"It's not about how hard you hit; it's about how hard you can get hit and keep moving forward."

—*Rocky Balboa*

You made it here, which means you've already done what most won't—and what almost none sustain. You didn't just light the match. You torched the status quo, danced on the ashes, and built something brave in its place. You found your spark and unleashed it like a freakin' flamethrower. But now? Now comes the final shackles you have to learn to throw off—the burnout, the boredom, the bureaucratic beast trying to snuff your flame.

What do you do when the adrenaline wears off and your revolution starts to feel like a calendar full of Tuesday meetings? When your passion feels like a pile of ash, and the system—sly bastard that it is—starts whispering again, "Go back to sleep. . ."

This chapter isn't some motivational poster nonsense. This is the heart of your war manual. Your blueprint for staying lit when everything around you is trying to dim your shine. Burnout? It isn't a glitch. It's a feature. It's the machine's last-ditch chokehold to force you back into the box you already smashed. But here's the truth: A real rebel doesn't just burn bright. A real rebel learns how to *refuel*—again and again and again.

This is about the dogged pursuit of new horizons. It's about cultivating hunger, curiosity, and friction. It's about breaking your own mold—over and over—before it crystallizes into comfort. It's not about how high you flame out. It's about building a system around you that serves as your ongoing ignition source so your light stays lit long after the parade's over.

No, I never said this was gonna be easy. But if you've made it this far, you already know—it's absolutely worth it.

**THE DRONE SHOT: A GHOST IN MY OWN LIFE**

Let me tell you something people don't like to admit: Even a life set on fire can start to smolder. I know, because mine almost did.

There was a stretch—gray, colorless, soul-sucking—when I felt like a freakin' hologram in my own life. Haunted. Hollowed out.

On paper, things were golden: a fresh paycheck, new zip code, shiny apartment, spotless new ride—really, a gilded cage. Underneath . . . I was dying. Not in a dramatic, sob story way. In a *quiet*, ever-eroding way. I had become the worst kind of ghost—the kind that keeps showing up.

Let's rewind to the cubicle gig that kickstarted my career. Six months in, and I was already running on fumes. I'd left Chicago behind, but the tears I cried on that outbound flight never really dried. I was lonely. I was untethered. And every day started to feel like déjà vu with a side of corporate jargon. I had climbed a ladder I didn't even remember pulling out and leaning against the wall.

Then came *that* moment.

I pulled into the office park one morning, stepped out of my car—and *boom*. It hit me like a sucker punch. The world slowed. The camera in my head zoomed out like a slow-motion drone shot in a dystopian movie. I saw myself, just another pixel in a soulless grid, walking toward a glass tower that didn't know my name and wouldn't register my disappearance. It was a vision of a life so small it might as well have been a clerical error. The sameness of it all—the bright white hallways, the scripted small talk, the flickering fluorescents—was like standing inside a mausoleum for ambition.

That day I felt it in my bones: If I didn't do something, I was gonna flatline. And then—just as quickly—I snapped out of it.

Maybe it was the way the security guard smiled that morning, like a human glitch in the matrix. Maybe I'd just had it with counting the same highway mile markers on my commute. All I know is something in me roared awake. Not a whisper—a *war cry*. I was done sleepwalking. Done swallowing boredom like it was normal. I wasn't okay with feeling numb. Not anymore.

Every step I took toward the building that day felt different, weighted, electric, *defiant*. That was the moment my rebellion began. One fierce, unglamorous choice: do whatever it takes to widen the crack of inertia.

And I did.

I started saying *yes* to anything that felt even remotely alive. Joined nonprofit boards and dove in headfirst. Asked sticky questions. Showed up at every food drive, 5K (walked it—no shame), school supply giveaway. I stuffed my weeknights with art shows, dinner parties, hip-hop nights, perfecting a new recipe. I dove into learning—and teaching—and somewhere along the way, "prof" became one of my favorite names to be called.

I stopped waiting to feel inspired and started living on purpose. Sucking the marrow out of life. On mission. On *fire*.

That drone-shot moment didn't end my story. It *rewrote* it.

It reminded me that staying sparked is a daily rebellion. That lightning in a bottle isn't some rare, magical thing you wait around for—it's the byproduct of movement, meaning, and choosing not to settle. Again and again.

So, here's your mandate: Feed the embers. Hunt new horizons. Break your own routine before it breaks you. This isn't about chasing the next high—it's about building a life that refuses to dim.

And if you're gonna burn . . . then burn on purpose.

**THE FADING FLAME: WHEN REBELS LOSE THEIR WAY**

Let's be real: The biggest threat to a sparked leader isn't some flashy new competitor or bureaucratic villain. It's something far more sinister. It's a sickness from within: stagnation. That slow, silent killer that creeps in when you stop feeding your fire. When you stop learning. Stop evolving. Stop getting uncomfortable. When the same rebel who once broke the system becomes the one upholding it . . . *because it benefits them now*.

The truth? The moment you start believing your own hype is the moment your flame starts to fade. History's littered with the corpses of once-iconic leaders, brands, and movements that flamed out—not because someone beat them but because they sat back, popped champagne, and stopped doing the real work.

Take BlackBerry. Yeah, *that* BlackBerry. At one point, they were untouchable, the kings of corporate cool. QWERTY keyboard, encrypted email, suits in every C-suite addicted to their little black bricks. (And drones like me too . . . "crackberry" was a real thing!) Their leaders were so drunk on their own dominance, they laughed off the iPhone like it was a toy. But here's the thing: While they were busy clinging to their past, Apple was building the future. And by the time BlackBerry woke up? It was over. Not with a bang but with a slow, embarrassing whisper into irrelevance. They didn't lose because someone hit harder—they lost because they *stopped moving forward*.

This isn't just a corporate cautionary tale—it happens in creative spaces all the time.

Think of all the artists who blow our minds once, then spend the rest of their careers recycling that moment. Afraid to change. Addicted to applause. Creatively zombified by the formula that once made them great.

Look at M. Night Shyamalan. *The Sixth Sense* was a cultural reset. It flipped the script on what a genre film could do. He was hailed as the next Hitchcock—a true visionary. But then came the echo chamber. The self-replication. *The Village. Lady in the Water.* Every film became a "wait for it . . ." twist that people could see coming a mile away. The rebel who once shocked the system became a parody of himself. His gift became his gimmick. His brilliance became a cage, and his reputation suffered because he failed to challenge his own success. He didn't just lose his way; he became trapped by his own genius until he was forced to blow it all up and start fresh.

Now let's talk about Marc Webb. Before superheroes swallowed him whole, he gave us *500 Days of Summer,* a rom-com with teeth, heart, and nonlinear swagger (and one of my personal faves!). It was vulnerable, experimental, human. Pure creative rebellion. Hollywood noticed, handed him superhero tights, and dropped him into the blockbuster blender. He directed the *Amazing Spider-Man* movies, the ones with Andrew Garfield. Financially, they did fine. Artistically? *Meh.* (Hot take—I know, I know!) The very thing that made him special—his daring narrative style, his emotional core—was scrubbed out in favor of CGI spectacle and box office "strategy." He got lost in the machine, forgetting the raw storytelling muscle that made him matter in the first place. And just like that, the rebel became a temporary star but a permanent pawn.

Remember Lena Dunham? The "it" girl writer/director/actor who took over our consciousness for a moment with her breakout show *Girls*? That seismic, raw, and genre-defining TV show was all everyone seemed to be talking about for a minute. But after the initial acclaim came backlash—criticism for being tone-deaf, privileged, and stuck in a narrow creative lens. For a while, it looked like her spark had dimmed. But Dunham didn't disappear. She recalibrated. She stepped behind the camera more often, took on new writing projects, and expanded her voice through more nuanced, inclusive storytelling. Her point of view might still be ultra-focused, but her path reminds us that sometimes the most rebellious thing you can do is listen, evolve, and keep creating—quietly, differently, but still lit from within.

Think Donald Glover. Actor. Rapper. Writer. Director. Comedian. His rebellion isn't singular—it's multidimensional. He refuses to be one thing, and by doing so, he remains everything—unpredictable, magnetic, unforgettable.

Glover didn't wait for permission to cross genres—he demolished the walls between them. He went from writing jokes on *30 Rock* to starring in sitcoms like *Community* to creating the genre-defying *Atlanta*, a surrealist meditation on race, fame, and American absurdity. As *Childish Gambino*, he dropped the searing "This Is America," a cultural gut punch that obliterated expectations of what a "rapper" should be. One moment he's in *Star Wars*, the next he's directing music videos or developing groundbreaking TV projects. He reinvents not because he has to—but because he refuses to calcify.

While others cling to formulas, Glover thrives in chaos. His superpower? Creative discomfort. He chases friction, reinvention, and evolution like oxygen. And in doing so, he's built a body of work that can't be boxed in, copied, or forgotten.

His rebellion is living proof—the most dangerous thing you can be is free. And freedom? It's earned in the crucible of constant evolution. His evolution isn't just art. It's armor. Which brings us to the myth that traps too many rebels.

Success is not the finish line. It's a trapdoor.

And if you're not careful, you'll fall through it into a pit of comfort, coasting, and creative decay. For sparked leaders, *impact* is the measure. *Evolution* is the path. *Hunger* is the posture.

The moment you stop chasing new horizons is the moment your fire starts to die. Don't let the view from your current mountain make you forget there are peaks still waiting to be climbed. Because the fuel that got you here? It won't keep you here.

You have to earn your spark every single day.

## THE LIE OF ARRIVAL

Time for a truth bomb: There is no "made it."

I'm proud of what I've built—of the risks I've taken, the impact I've made, the sparks I've lit along the way. And yeah, sometimes I pause and take it all in. I let it hit me: *Damn. We did that.* That reflection? That internal celebration? It's earned.

But those are also the moments when I'm most grateful for my crew—the insiders who keep me grounded even when the altitude gets high. They're not there to dim the glow but to remind me this fire isn't finished.

Because "Have I made it?" is the wrong question. Once you answer that, you stop climbing. You stop pushing. You trade your fire for comfort. Your edge for applause.

And that's how leaders become monuments—admired but motionless.

The cultural myth of *arrival* is seductive—that once you've achieved enough, earned enough, won enough . . . you can exhale. Coast. But sparked leaders know better. Fulfillment isn't found in arrival—it lives in motion. In reinvention. In refusing to be defined by a single victory.

Take Kobe Bryant. Five-time NBA champ. Basketball legend. He could've taken his trophies and faded into quiet luxury. But instead, he reignited. He built Granity Studios, poured himself into storytelling, and won an Oscar for *Dear Basketball*. He didn't retire. He reloaded.

Michelle Obama? She redefined the role of First Lady. But when that chapter closed, she didn't disappear into legacy. She launched a global book tour, *The Light We Carry*, using storytelling as medicine—for herself and for millions. She shifted the stage, not the spark.

These weren't nostalgia tours. They were evolutions. New mountains. New heat.

So yes, celebrate your wins. Toast your breakthroughs. But don't settle into arrival. That's not your story.

You're a sparked leader.
The hustle doesn't end.
It morphs. Deepens. Sharpens.

*You're not here to make it.*
You're here to keep making it matter.

**SEASONS OF FIRE**

Before we move into some strategic arrows you can add into your quiver, let's talk about rhythm. And to do that, we need to pause for a moment.

Take a breath. Roll your shoulders. You've been running hot. But even the fiercest flames need rhythm. Without it, they don't just fade—they collapse.

You are not a spark machine. You're a human being with cycles, shifts, and evolution. So let's name them.

These aren't steps on a ladder. They're seasons in a cycle. Each one has power. Each one has purpose.

**Spring (Ignition) – Fuel the Spark**
This one's a blast. It's all fresh energy and big dreams. The curiosity is loud, the optimism runs deep, and you're hungry. Maybe it's the start of your career. Maybe it's a full-blown reinvention. Either way, you're new here, and that's a superpower.

I've lived this more than once—starting in journalism, jumping to higher ed, dabbling in nonprofit, bouncing into corporate, then hopping back to brand storytelling, with a pitstop in strategy. Every pivot was a fresh spring.

In this season, your job is to absorb.
Soak it all in.
Read everything.
Say yes more than no.

Let the spark wander until it finds a flame.

**Summer (Expansion) – Build the Bonfire**
This is the stretch-and-grow season. You're hitting your stride and building muscle—skills, stamina, and swagger. It's time to go full-stack—deepen your expertise, broaden your toolkit.

Take a course. Get certified. Shadow someone smarter. Ask questions like your life depends on it. Build your personal brand.

This is when your fire turns from flicker to blaze.

But remember: Expansion without intention is chaos. You're not chasing everything—you're constructing something.

**Fall (Reflection) – Burn with Wisdom**

At some point, people start looking to you. Asking for advice. Quoting your words. Watching how you move. You've become the sage. Welcome to fall.

Now's the time to say less and mean more. To respond instead of react. To lead with intentionality, not urgency.

And yes—this is the season of boundaries. You've earned the right to say no. To choose your table. To preserve your fire.

Let your wisdom linger like smoke in the air. Present, powerful, and impossible to ignore.

**Winter (Stillness) – Tend the Embers**

Winter isn't burnout. It's a recalibration. It's the slow, necessary lull before the next spark. Maybe you're handing off the reins, mentoring the next wave. Maybe you're going quiet to dream bigger. Either way, this season is sacred.

Stillness doesn't mean you've stopped mattering. It means you're choosing how to matter next.

Winter is when reinvention sneaks in through the cracks. A quieter fire. A steadier pace. A return to essence. And when you choose to engage—it lands harder.

So don't fear this season.<br>
Own it.<br>
Rest in it.<br>
Reimagine from it.

**Final Thought**

Not all fires roar. Some simmer. Some flicker. Some smolder with quiet intensity.

But as long as your fire still lives—you're not done.

**THE SPARKED PLAYBOOK FOR LONGEVITY**

Okay, now let's figure out how to sustain the unquenchable fire of a sparked leader without burning out.

Start by realizing that longevity isn't about white-knuckling your way through leadership. It's not about working longer hours, chasing bigger titles, or racking up more achievements like it's some kind of résumé arms race. It's about intentional, relentless, soul-deep growth. It's about rebellion turned ritual. It's about becoming the kind of leader who evolves faster than the system can box them in.

Here's your *Sparked* survival kit: four battle-tested strategies to help you stay dangerous, relevant, and *deeply motivated* for the long haul.

**1. Make Learning a Lifestyle (Not a Checklist)**

A sparked leader knows that your brain is your sharpest weapon, and *curiosity* is your eternal fuel source.

- **Burn the Syllabus.** Learning isn't confined to a lecture hall. It doesn't end when you hang up your diploma. It's in the podcast that makes you rethink your assumptions. It's in that Friday night doc that hits harder than expected. I've learned as much about leadership in a random, late-night convo about supply chains with a Lyft driver as I have from a business book. *Everything* is curriculum if you pay attention.

- **Mentor Like You Mean It (Both Ways).** Get yourself a circle of wise, unfiltered mentors who challenge your ego and expand your map. Then *become* one. Teaching forces you to articulate your beliefs, evolve your frameworks, and notice your own blind spots in real time. That's rebel reciprocity.
- **Unlearn or Die.** Seriously. The habits that made you successful last year might be the very thing holding you back this year. Don't just collect knowledge—*shed it*. Break up with outdated beliefs. Deconstruct your sacred cows. Stay humble enough to question your own gospel. This is a humbling yet essential act of self-rebellion.

**2. Stretch Till It Stings**

Growth doesn't come from comfort. It comes from friction, fear, and failing forward with your sleeves rolled up. To avoid stagnation, you must constantly put yourself in new, uncomfortable situations. It's in these moments of friction that new neural pathways are formed, and your rebel lens is sharpened.

- **Jump Into the Deep End.** Take on projects that make you sweat. If you're a systems nerd, dive into something wildly creative. If you live in strategy, go lead execution. Let your identity get convoluted—you'll come out sharper, scrappier, and more valuable than ever. These experiences force you to build new skills and see your role from a fresh perspective.
- **Crash a New Party.** Insert yourself into a new space—a nonprofit board (worked for me!), a dance class, a faith-based hackathon, a community garden. Different people, different norms, different rules. You'll flex muscles you didn't know you had and sharpen ones

you've been neglecting. Each new environment comes with its own set of rules, challenges, and people, all of which will stretch your cognitive and interpersonal skills.

- **Travel to Get Lost.** Don't just vacation—disrupt. Go somewhere that flips your internal compass upside down. Get lost, get awkward, mispronounce things, and get laughed at. There's no growth hack like cultural disorientation. I've learned more about flexibility and communication from being lost in a foreign country than from any corporate training course. It rewires your adaptability like nothing else.

**3. Adapt or Be Forgotten**

Rebels don't just surf the waves—they *create* them. If you want to stay in the game, you have to stay *tuned in* and *turned on* to the world that's constantly in flux.

- **Fall in Love with the Unknown.** Obsess over what's coming next—AI, climate shifts, Gen Z's worldview, the death of email, the rise of micro-communities . . . Don't just read headlines—*interrogate* them. Ask yourself, "How will this change the world I'm trying to build?" The future doesn't reward the best résumé. It rewards the sharpest antenna.
- **Diversify Your Feed—Religiously.** As we learned in Chapter 6, your greatest asset is the diversity of your inputs. Follow people who piss you off, read books in genres you "don't like," listen to voices that live outside your bubble. This isn't about being woke—it's about being *awake*. Fresh inputs create fresh insights. Period.

- **Audit Your Inner Compass.** A life of constant rebellion won't happen by accident. You must build in time for reflection. Stop and ask: *Am I still leading from my heretic purpose? Am I still awake in the work—or just going through the motions?* Calibrate often. Rebel hard. Course-correct fast. Complacency is a killer dressed in comfort.

**4. Roll Deep with Rebels**

Lone wolf rebels burn out. The sharpest ones roll deep—with a crew that tells them the truth, pulls them higher, and refuses to let them settle.

- **Curate Your Circle Like Your Life Depends on It—Because It Does.** You need people around you who won't just clap for your success but who will call out your slip-ups. Friends who see your potential and won't let you waste it. Colleagues who ask better questions. Mentors who pull no punches. Co-conspirators who dream as boldly as you do.
- **Choose Friction Over Flattery.** Echo chambers are easy. Challenge is sacred. Find people who argue with you—not to win but to *sharpen*. Iron sharpens iron, but only if it's allowed to grind.
- **Grow Together or Grow Apart.** Build relationships with people who are just as obsessed with becoming better as you are. Schedule "deep dive" dinners. Host idea labs. Trade feedback like oxygen. Fuel each other's flames. *Your spark was never meant to burn in isolation.*

**The Final Word**

Longevity doesn't come from coasting. It comes from a daily decision to ignite again. To stretch again. To question again. To surround yourself with people who refuse to let your brilliance go dim. Your crew is your flint—strike often, spark more.

Your next horizon is waiting—but only if you stay in motion.

So if you're gonna burn . . . burn in motion. Burn with meaning. Burn like it matters.

**THE SPARK PLUG:**

**Arianna Huffington – The Audacious Pivot**

Our spark plug for this chapter is Arianna Huffington, the visionary leader who proved that a personal crisis could be a springboard for a revolutionary new idea. For years, she was a titan of digital media, co-founding *The Huffington Post* and embodying the nonstop "hustle culture" that dominates modern leadership. She worked eighteen-hour days, slept very little, and constantly pushed for more. This frantic pace was a core part of the company's early success, but it came at a profound cost.

The turning point came in 2007 when, exhausted and sleep-deprived, she collapsed at her desk, breaking her cheekbone. This severe, physical manifestation of burnout was a profound wake-up call, forcing her to confront not only her personal unsustainable pace but also the systemic flaws in modern work culture she had helped create. Instead of viewing her collapse as a personal failure, she made an audacious pivot, transforming her crisis into a powerful new mission. She became a vocal advocate for well-being and sleep, authoring the best-selling book *Thrive* and founding Thrive Global, a company dedicated to ending the burnout epidemic. Her journey demonstrates that a leader's longevity isn't about how hard they work but how wisely they manage their energy. She showed the world that a struggle, embraced with purpose, can ignite a revolutionary new idea and an enduring influence that burns far brighter than the relentless grind.

Her pivot wasn't just a personal evolution—it was a systemic rebellion. She redefined hustle, shattered the myth of burnout as a badge of honor, and lit a movement that made rest revolutionary.

**GET SPARKED:**

**The Personal Re-Ignition Plan**

Rebellious leadership is a marathon, not a sprint. To sustain your fire, you must actively and consciously seek out new sources of ignition. This exercise is designed to help you create a plan to do just that.

**The Prompt:**

Rebellious leadership can be exhausting. To sustain your "fire," what's one area of your personal or professional life where you feel stagnant or comfortable? Identify one new skill, one unfamiliar experience, or one radically different perspective you will intentionally explore this quarter. This isn't for a specific work goal but purely to "re-spark" your own curiosity, reinvigorate your adaptability, and broaden your rebel lens.

**Your Challenge:**

- **Identify the Stagnation:** In what part of your life do you feel the most "rinse and repeat" lately? Be honest.

- **Choose Your Spark:** Pick a new skill, a new experience, or a new perspective to explore. This should be something that makes you slightly uncomfortable or curious.
- **Define Your First Step:** What is the one small, concrete, and immediate action you will take in the next forty-eight hours to begin this journey (e.g., download a new podcast, enroll in a free online course, schedule a coffee with someone from a different industry)?

**Thought to Spark On:**

The greatest leaders don't just inspire others; they make sure they don't lose their own flame. What will you do to keep your fire burning?

# PART IV

# LEAVE LIGHT BEHIND

*The long arc of rebellious leadership—beyond accolades and into legacy.*

# CHAPTER 9

# THE LEGACY OF LIGHT: FORGING A LIFE THAT BLAZES FIERCELY BEYOND YOU

"What we do in life, echoes in eternity."

—*Gladiator*

So here we are. You've stoked the fire within. You've sparked others to rise. You've rattled outdated systems and dared to defy the playbook. Now comes the final provocation: *Will your impact die with you? Or will it burn wild, untamed, and contagious long after you're gone?*

That's the question. The one that should haunt and thrill any sparked leader who has chosen to build something bold, fierce, and alive in the world. You don't get to pick the day you leave the room. But you do get to decide what still echoes after you're gone.

Let me put it plainly: If the revolution ends with you, it wasn't a revolution. It was a performance.

This final chapter isn't about legacy in the polite, boardroom sense of the word. This is about leaving a mark they can't scrub off the walls. This is about becoming so radically clear, so unmistakably *you*, that your presence haunts institutions in the best possible way—provoking courage, demanding justice, sparking movement. Legacy isn't what you leave behind neatly folded; it's what you set ablaze and dare others to keep feeding.

Forget statues. Forget plaques. This is about *people* . . . the ones you've awakened, challenged, empowered. The ones now bold enough to call BS when they see it. The ones who learned from you how to build, destroy, rebuild, and lead from within.

To spark that kind of generational momentum, you have to go all in. Lead with brutal transparency. Invite voices that shake the table. Build systems that outgrow you. And then *get out of the damn way.*

This is servant leadership with gasoline. This is humility with heat. This is the moment when you stop asking, *What will they remember about me?*, and start asking, *Who will rise because of me?*

Ready to finish what you started?

It's time to let it burn.

## FUELING A FIRE THAT OUTLASTS YOU

Let's be real—the craving to leave a mark? It's rarely noble at first. It's ego in a purpose costume. But a sparked leader grows the hell up. They realize legacy isn't about their name echoing in boardrooms or plaques with their photo in a dusty hallway.

It's about *others*—fueled, unleashed, and wildly alive because of how they led.

If your legacy starts and ends with *you*, it was never that deep to begin with.

A true rebel legacy is embedded, not branded. It's not about owning the spotlight. It's about passing the freaking torch—so others light their own fires and torch the status quo in ways you never imagined. That means your leadership isn't about control. It's about catalytic empowerment. You're not the centerpiece. You're the accelerant.

## RADICAL HONESTY IN A FILTERED WORLD

In a world drowning in curated perfection, being real is revolutionary. Transparency isn't weakness—it's a weapon. It slashes through the crap and says, "Here's where we really are. Now let's build something true."

- **Share the Why, Not Just the What:** Plans are cheap. Stories are currency. Your people don't want another memo. They want to know *why it matters*. When announcing a new direction, a sparked leader doesn't just state the plan. They tell the story of how they got there. They share the friction. The fear. The breakthroughs. They let people into the messy middle where real decisions are made. This invites others to engage with the reasoning, not just the outcome. It transforms them from passive recipients of a plan to active partners in a mission.
- **Acknowledge Uncertainty:** You're not omniscient, and pretending to be just makes you look insecure. Say "I don't know"—and mean it. Then say, "Let's figure it

out." That's how trust is built in the rubble. Admit what you don't know and invite your team to help you figure it out. This builds trust and transforms a top-down mandate into a collaborative mission.

- **Be a Human, Not a Hero:** No one follows a cardboard cutout. Show your bruises. Share the time you blew it. Own the L. That's the stuff that creates psychological safety and opens up a space where others *dare* to try. Your team doesn't need a flawless leader; they need a human one. Share a story of a personal setback or a decision that didn't work out. This models resilience and intellectual honesty, creating a culture where it's safe for everyone to take risks and learn from their mistakes.

**BUILD THE ROOM, THEN BURN THE SCRIPT**

Your heretic purpose is a powerful engine, but it runs on more than just your personal fuel.

Command and control is dead. Co-creation is the revolution.

You don't build a movement by shouting orders. You build it by issuing invitations so bold people can't ignore them. You say, "I've got a dream. Wanna make it wilder with me?" A true sparked leader is a master of invitation, actively drawing in diverse ideas and perspectives to strengthen their vision. You don't just open a suggestion box; you create a compelling reason for others to jump into the sandbox with you.

- **Structure for Co-Creation:** Your meetings aren't meetings. They're underground labs for creative rebellion. Kill the agenda. Light a spark. Rethink your collaborative spaces. Instead of using meetings as a place to hand down assignments, use them as "change labs" where you pose a challenge and ask for wild ideas. Tools like design-thinking workshops, hackathons, or even a simple whiteboard session with a bold prompt can make co-creation feel less like a chore and more like a creative act. Pose questions so provocative it makes everyone in the room sit up straight. "What would it look like to blow this up and rebuild it better?"

- **Democratize Dialogue:** Stop waiting for the extroverts. Seek out the quiet powerhouses in the room. The most reserved person can sometimes have the most disruptive idea. A sparked leader makes a point to ask for their input directly, creating a space where everyone's unique perspective is not just welcome but expected. Pull the genius out of the overlooked and underestimated. Let the misfits speak—and then *shut up and listen*.
- **Build Your "Inner Circle" of Difference:** If everyone around you agrees with you, congrats—you've built a cult, not a legacy. Find your friction crew. The ones who push back, see sideways, and make your ideas sharper. Your core team shouldn't be an echo chamber of your own thinking but a rich kaleidoscope of insights. This is how you avoid blind spots and build solutions that resonate with a wider world.

## DIALOGUE OVER DECREE: CULTIVATE A CULTURE THAT DOESN'T NEED YOU

Legacy isn't your final act. It's your disappearing trick. The moment you've built something so alive, so self-generating that it doesn't need you anymore—*that's the mic drop.* This means moving from a leadership style of decree—where you give orders—to one of dialogue, where you ask questions and empower others to find the answers.

- **Lead with Dangerous Questions:** Forget the "how." Ask, "What's the sacred cow we need to slaughter?" or "What would our fiercest competitor never dare to do—but we just might?" Make your people think so big they get scared. Then help them do it anyway. This shifts the ownership of the solution from you to the team, a crucial step in building their confidence and expertise.
- **Make Dialogue the Default:** Ditch the town halls and start hosting truth circles. Regular, unfiltered, casual conversations. Walk and talks. Coffee collisions. That's how trust grows roots. Dialogue shouldn't be reserved for big moments; it needs to be an everyday practice. This builds the trust and psychological safety needed for a team to perform at its peak.
- **Celebrate What *Most* Leaders Fear:** Failure. Messy pivots. Wobbly first steps. Praise the process, not just the win. Honor the try. That's how you turn your culture into an engine of invention that outlives your leadership. By framing every outcome as a chance for growth, you build a culture of resilience and continuous improvement, ensuring your rebellious philosophy lives on in your team's DNA. This is how you forge a life that blazes fiercely beyond you.

Putting all these insights together really begins to catalyze when you realize that a sparked leader's greatest success is in the inspired and changed lives of those they get to guide. Pouring all that you have learned into those around you is the true mark of success.

We call this mentorship.

**THE ILLUSION OF THE STATUE**

I serve on a couple of nonprofit boards these days, which still blows my mind. The kid from the hood, now being invited to the table like some kind of elder statesman. Not what fourteen-year-old me would have imagined. But here we are.

On one of those boards, maybe the most prestigious one, I learned quickly that board service isn't just about your brilliance. It's also about your bank account. That was a humbling wake-up call. Some folks are there because they can fund the vision. Others, like me, are there to shape it.

But here's the thing: When you contribute, you also get the chance to be recognized. A name on a building. A plaque. An award. For some leaders, this is the height of achievement.

For sparked leaders? That's the knockoff version of legacy. Hollow compared to the legacy they create through people they ignite, the systems they rewire, and the sparks they spread.

Full disclosure: Nothing's named after me. No statues. No wings of a building. But I've had the privilege of mentoring over two dozen fierce, purposeful young people. They know who they are. And I know the mark they'll leave. That's the legacy I care about.

Too many leaders are chasing the statue, not the spark. They want their legacy etched in marble.

Sparked leaders want theirs etched in people.

I once worked on a consulting assignment with Uber, back in the Travis Kalanick era. I didn't interact with him directly—thankfully—but I felt the ripples of his reputation. Kalanick had built a dominant personal brand. But he also built a culture that was toxic, cutthroat, and unsustainable. His name may have been associated with the brand, and the kudos for the company's success were attributed to him, but when the board forced him out to preserve the company, none of that mattered, did it?

No matter how big your name, if the system you lead is built on fear, ego, or dysfunction—it won't last. The brand might survive. But the damage endures.

Sparked leaders don't chase bronze busts or legacy lounges. They lead with this truth: "What we do in life echoes in eternity." They don't aim for immortality. They aim for *impact*. Not because it's tidy. Not because it'll always be recognized. But because they know the fire they light in others burns longer than any statue ever will.

**THE UNSUNG FOUNDER WHO SPARKED GENERATIONS**

One of the clearest examples of sparked legacy in action is the Reverend Dr. Alfonso Wyatt. In New York civic and nonprofit circles, Dr. Wyatt is legend. Nationally? Many have never heard of him. And that's part of what makes him such a profound example.

He didn't chase a public profile. He built a pipeline.

For over two decades as VP at the Fund for the City of New York, Dr. Wyatt strengthened youth-serving organizations and mentored three full generations of leaders. From foster youth to doctoral students, he seeded greatness quietly, patiently, deliberately.

He founded Strategic Destiny to connect faith with data, evidence with vision. He helped establish the Institute for Transformative Mentoring and the Credible Messenger Institute—pioneering efforts that gave legitimacy and funding to programs that raised up justice-impacted individuals as leaders.

This wasn't splashy work. It was systemic, slow, and soul deep.

Dr. Wyatt shows us that sparked legacy isn't built on applause. It's built on intentional, relational power transfer. On designing systems that carry forward without your presence. On never being the ceiling to someone else's rise.

**THE SPARK ONLY YOU CAN GIVE**

Not every legacy story ends with a headline. In fact, most don't. Dr. Wyatt reminds us that real legacy lives in motion—in systems, institutions, and people set in motion by one spark. I've seen that spark up close. Twice, in fact. And it changed everything for me.

My time at NBC News was a crash course in the value of mentorship, and I was fortunate enough to be taken under the wing of two veteran producers who taught me so much in vastly different yet equally foundational ways.

Let me take you back. I was twenty-five. Hungry. Eyes wide. Absolutely green. The air was electric—phones ringing off the hook at the assignment desk, police scanners chirping away, news updates being written and passed around for edits, and screens everywhere capturing everything happening all around the world. Reporters ran for elevators on their way to assignments; anchorpeople were on set delivering the latest newscast; writers and producers were crafting the latest updates. Then *bam*—Teddy.

Old school. Trenchcoat vibes. A journalism legend who had done it all, seen it all, and met them all. Really! He served as bureau chief in Frankfurt, Germany; Paris France; and Moscow, USSR. Whenever NBC hired new correspondents, they were assigned to learn the ropes with Teddy. He guided many journalistic luminaries: Judy Woodruff, Gwen Ifill, Anne Thompson, David Gregory, and Brian Williams. And now, he was making time for me! (I got to work with each of them. And I'll never forget the time I saved a live shot for Gwen Ifill by offering her the literal earrings off my ears before she went live on national television. It wasn't a sparked leadership lesson, but it sure as hell sparked my excitement for being fully present, fully useful, fully alive in the moment. Sometimes leadership looks like presence. Period.)

Teddy had history written into the lines on his face. He didn't baby me. He didn't spoon-feed me. He let me witness greatness up close. That was the gift. Exposure.

I sat beside him in edit rooms as he sliced a story like a scalpel. I watched him interview giants and turn dense history into soul-stirring narrative. Watching him work was a masterclass in time-tested technique. I learned not just *how* to do the work but how to *think* like a journalist—curious, prepared, full of grit.

Then came Eric.

Whereas Teddy was the rumpled older newshound, Eric was the young superstar making a name at NBC. He was Brokaw's go-to producer, always working on the high-profile newsmaker stories. He was a polished, modern, fast-talking, fast-thinking antithesis to Teddy.

Teddy *showed* me the work. Eric *included* me in it.

He loved sharing his wisdom, his tips, his tricks. He always made time for my questions—as many questions as I wanted to ask—and always had time for a constructive response that helped me learn something new. I was able to ask the "dumb" questions and always felt the safety of his support and his kind, guiding response toward the right answers. It always started with warmth—"Okay, pal."

He would reposition me during a shoot so I could appreciate the same point of view he had discovered. He allowed me to make choices in the edit room so that I could feel the weight of the decisions and struggle with the pace needed for success. Eric was the player-coach who had every right to ignore me—and didn't. He *welcomed* the questions. He pulled me into the process. Gave me room to stumble and still had my back.

Those two men *shaped me*. Not by giving me answers but by creating the conditions where I could become my own kind of force. That's mentorship. That's legacy.

You want legacy? It's not built in your résumé. It's embedded in the souls you light up along the way.

## TRANSFERRING THE FLAME

The question isn't whether you'll leave. You will. The question is: When you go, does anything burn on?

That's why we develop people, not personas. That's why we systematize values, not just vibes. That's why sparked leaders care less about credit and more about continuity.

Which brings us to the unsung variable in legacy: your crew.

## YOUR LEGACY LIVES IN THEIR MOUTHS

Back when I was leading a brand storytelling initiative for a Fortune 500 client, I found myself face-to-face with R&B star and *Fast & Furious* actor Tyrese Gibson. He was in comeback mode—top of the charts with *Stay* and still hot off the heels of blockbuster stardom. We were filming content for a brand campaign, and I was in charge—directing the session, conducting the interview, showing up as the cool, confident leader I thought I was.

Turns out, not so much.

And Tyrese let me know. Immediately.

***Me:*** *It's been a minute. How will the fans know you've still got it?*
***Tyrese:*** *Motherf*#%!! Do you know who I am?*
***Me (gulp):*** *I mean . . . do they?*
***Tyrese:*** *Who do you want me to call? Ri Ri? Beyoncé? Let's settle this now.*

He grabbed his phone and held it up like a mic drop.

I froze. My team didn't.

That's when my trusted deputy—my buddy AK—stepped in to smooth things over. (Honestly, she was always the cooler one.) Later that day, in a private debrief, she gave it to me straight. No fluff. No soft landing. Just facts. I had overplayed the chill.

Missed the moment to connect. AK didn't shame me—but she didn't sugarcoat it either. And because of our years of trust and rhythm, I could hear it, own it, and grow from it.

Thanks to her quick thinking in the moment—and her honesty after the fact—we salvaged the shoot and the story.

That's the power of a *real* crew.

Not just the ones who stand beside you when the cameras are rolling—but the ones who speak up when the lights go out. Who tell the truth in the private rooms. Who shape, not just protect, your legacy.

Here's how to build your own crew that sharpens your spark and carries your name with truth:

**1. Don't confuse a hype squad with a legacy crew.**
Hype is fun. We all love the people who gas us up.

But a legacy crew? They're the ones who tell the truth—even when it stings. They challenge fuzzy thinking. Check your ego. Hold up a mirror, not a spotlight.

If you're serious about impact, surround yourself with people who are empowered to push back, ask better questions, and call you forward. And here's the beautiful twist: Those are also the people whose praise hits the deepest—because it's not performative. It's earned.

**2. Watch for the legacy-blockers.**
Every room has a few. The chronic doubters. The status quo defenders. The folks who only clap when there's a camera around—or worse, the ones trying to build their empire off your work.

Here's who I've learned to spot:

- The "yes (to your face) but nah (behind your back)" people
- The oxygen thieves who hijack the moment
- The peacocks who repost your wins but never build with you

Sparked leadership isn't naive. It's generous, yes. But it's not gullible. Trust your gut. If someone's presence costs you clarity, momentum, or purpose, they're not crew . . . they're driftwood.

**3. Create rituals that reinforce reflection and reciprocity.** Legacy doesn't happen by accident. You build it. And you build it in the *company* of others.

That awkward post-interview moment with Tyrese? It was a ritual for us—debriefs after every high-stake moment. Wins, fumbles, near misses. Not to perform excellence but to practice it. To learn out loud. To stay sharp.

- Schedule **quarterly "mirror moments"** with your crew —private, intentional check-ins where the goal is honesty, not ego.
- Build **public thank-you rituals.** Shout out the people behind the scenes. Normalize shared credit.
- Host **legacy circles**—small gatherings (IRL or in person) where your team revisits purpose, vision, and what's getting in the way.

Here's your TL;DR: Your legacy doesn't live in your résumé. It lives in the stories your crew says about you when you're not in the room.

Because here's the ordinary lie: Legacy is a solo performance, sculpted in marble and sealed with a mic drop. Sparked leaders know better. Legacy lives in movement, in mouths, in the stories that echo long after you're gone.

Make sure those words are rooted in respect, truth, and fire!

## LEAVING THE ROOM BETTER THAN YOU FOUND IT

Let's make this plain: If your impact dies when you log out or step down, you built a brand, *not* a legacy.

The *Sparked* legacy lives in systems, stories, and people that continue to spark others. It's about building a future, not just living in the present. This is the ultimate act of defiant leadership—the refusal to let your purpose end with you.

### In Business: Transforming a Giant with a Human-Centric Mission

Satya Nadella took over Microsoft at a time when the company was seen as a relic of the past, mired in a rigid, competitive internal culture and focused on defending its legacy products like Windows. Nadella's heretic purpose was to re-imagine the very identity of the tech giant. He introduced a new, purpose-driven philosophy centered on empathy and a "growth mindset," shifting the company's core mission from "a computer on every desk" to "empowering every person and every organization on the planet to achieve more."

This wasn't just a marketing slogan; it was a systemic change. He aggressively pivoted the company toward cloud computing (Azure) and open-source software, a move that went against decades of Microsoft's fiercely proprietary culture. He shattered internal silos and fostered a collaborative, "learn-it-all" culture, which was a radical departure from the previous "know-it-all" ethos.

By leading with purpose and empathy, Nadella transformed Microsoft from an inward-looking, slow-moving giant into an innovative, market-leading force, proving that even the most entrenched systems can be reshaped from within by a leader who dares to see the world through fresh eyes. His legacy is not just a successful business but a case study in how to reinvent a company's soul.

**In Entertainment: A Stage for All Voices**

Issa Rae, a master storyteller, has created a legacy that began not in a boardroom but on YouTube. Her journey from a hit web series, *The Misadventures of Awkward Black Girl*, to a premium television series, *Insecure*, and a production company, HOORAE, is a blueprint for how to rewrite the rules from the ground up. She actively championed and centered the stories of Black women who were often overlooked or reduced to stereotypes, demonstrating that a specific, authentic voice could have universal resonance.

Through her production company, she has intentionally created opportunities for other Black creators, writers, and directors, opening doors that were previously bolted shut. Her legacy is not just the hit shows she created but the generation of creators she empowered to tell their own stories, ensuring that the entertainment industry's narrative is more inclusive and authentic for decades to come.

**In Higher Education: A Model for the Future**

Ben Nelson, the visionary founder of Minerva University, created a legacy that is actively reshaping what higher education looks like for a new generation. He didn't accept the traditional university model—expensive, geographically bound, and lecture-focused—as the only way forward. He chose to rewrite the rules, not just through incremental change but through a total system reinvention.

Nelson's enterprising idea was to build a university with no physical campus. Instead, students rotate through seven different global cities, from San Francisco to Buenos Aires, throughout their four years. The curriculum is entirely project-based, a "flipped classroom" model where students learn through debate and active problem-solving, not passive lectures. This wasn't just a new school; it was a profound act of defiance, a bold claim that a global, practical, and highly selective education could be delivered without the traditional trappings of a campus.

His enduring impact is the institution he built that serves as a living, breathing testament to a heretic purpose, inspiring countless educators and students to believe that the boundaries of learning are only self-imposed and that with enough audacity, you can truly build a new reality.

**STOP DREAMING. START TORCHING.**

Another moment for clarity: *Legacy isn't later. Legacy is now.*

Every day that you wake up and choose courage over comfort, that's legacy. Every meeting where you challenge the lazy default, that's legacy. Every time you elevate another voice instead of your own, that's legacy.

So don't wait for your final chapter to start living like your life has meaning. *It already does.*

You've journeyed through the inner work of a sparked leader—unearthing your purpose, sharpening your lens, and taking the audacious leap. You've learned to fan those flames outward, igniting change in teams and communities. Now, as our final chapter closes, you stand at a crucial crossroads. This is where you decide if all these lessons remain just words on a page . . . or they become the fuel that propels your future.

The world doesn't need more managers of the status quo. It needs revolutionaries with a purpose. It needs leaders who are willing to reject the ordinary lie not just once but every single day. It needs you to recognize that your most powerful tool isn't your position or your title but your choices.

The legacy of light you forge isn't a distant aspiration; it's a daily practice. It's in the courage to speak up in a meeting, the empathy to listen to the unheard, and the audacity to try something new, even if you might fail. Your life is a story. But are you letting the world write it for you, or will you seize the pen and fill its pages with a blaze of your own making?

This is your final spark, your last dare, your whispered "hell yes" to everything ahead.

Legacy isn't what's left over—it's what gets lit while you're still alive. It's the torch you pass, the spark you plant, the system you leave trembling with potential.

Stop future-tripping. Light the match already. Be the friction. Be the firestarter. Be the rebel they'll thank later.

True legacy doesn't whisper—it positively explodes, leaving burn marks.

Let them talk about you like a hurricane. Let your impact arrive like thunder—unmistakable, wild, and never quite gone. Let them wonder how one person made the room feel like a revolution. Let your light be the one they can't unsee.

And when they ask what lit the fuse?

You'll smile.

You were the match.

**SPARK PLUG:**
**Boyan Slat (The Ocean Cleanup) – The Unwavering Compass**
Our final spark plug is Boyan Slat, the founder and CEO of The Ocean Cleanup. Conceived when he was just eighteen, after seeing more plastic than fish while diving in Greece, his idea wasn't a fleeting thought; it sparked a sustained, spirited rebellion against the deeply ingrained idea that the ocean plastic problem was simply too vast to tackle.

Slat didn't just create a nonprofit; he built a movement. The Ocean Cleanup develops and scales technologies to rid the world's oceans of plastic, with the bold goal of removing 90 percent of it by 2040. What's truly remarkable is that Slat doesn't just focus on the technology. He inspires countless others—in environmental activism, engineering, and entrepreneurship—to believe that massive, seemingly impossible challenges can be met with innovative, sustained effort. He has created a legacy of courageous hope, proving that a fierce commitment to a purpose, even one born from a seemingly small moment of inspiration, can mobilize global action and forge a path toward a cleaner, healthier planet for generations to come.

## GET SPARKED:

### The Unextinguishable Flame

True legacy isn't built for you; it's built through you. This final exercise is about moving from being a sparked leader to becoming a catalyst for a lasting movement—a movement that burns fiercely beyond your direct actions.

**The Prompt:**

Imagine your sparked leadership is a living flame that will continue to burn for generations.

**Your Challenge:**

- What are the three core principles or beliefs you would want that flame to illuminate for future leaders and the world? These are the non-negotiable truths of your purpose.
- Who, in your current sphere of influence, has the potential to carry a piece of that flame forward? Identify a mentee, a junior colleague, a family member, or a peer.
- Commit to one deliberate, small act of mentorship, empowerment, or shared action with that person in the next month. It could be a simple conversation, a door you open for them, or a piece of knowledge you deliberately pass on, ensuring your rebellious spirit continues to ignite beyond your direct actions.

**Thought to Spark On:**

The greatest leaders don't create followers; they create other leaders. What spark will you pass on?

# EPILOGUE

# THE SPARKED CREED

When it's all said and done . . .

Did you kick open the doors—and hold them wide for the ones coming next?
Did you *amplify* your light, not hoard it?
Did you speak truth even when—*especially* when—your voice shook?
Did you refuse the box, the label, the convenient half-version of yourself?
Did you make damn sure it was never just about you?

Were you more than a bystander in history's swirl?
Did you show up with fire in your chest and purpose in your stride?
Did you grow louder in love, bolder in action, fiercer in your convictions?
Did you let difference sharpen you—not scare you?
Did you stop waiting for permission and start building something wild?

Did you leave it *all* on the field—sweat, voice, soul, spark?

If so . . . then exhale. Let the match burn down.

Because the blaze lives on.
In the ones you challenged.
The ones you elevated.
The ones you dared to believe in.

You didn't just show up. You lit the fuse.

The fire's still raging.

You did that.

Make sure the ones coming next don't just inherit ashes.

www.ingramcontent.com/pod-product-compliance
Lightning Source LLC
Chambersburg PA
CBHW030918060726
47591CB00005B/1593

* 9 7 8 1 9 6 6 7 8 6 9 2 4 *